CLIMBING
THE
RAINBOW

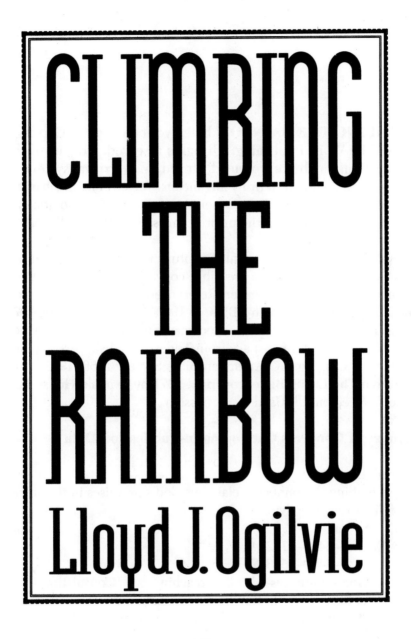

CLIMBING THE RAINBOW

Lloyd J. Ogilvie

WORD PUBLISHING

Dallas · London · Vancouver · Melbourne

Unless otherwise indicated, all Scripture references are from the New King James Version of the Bible, copyright © 1979, 1980, 1982, Thomas Nelson, Inc., Publisher. References indicated NASB are from the New American Standard Bible © 1960, 1962, 1963, 1968, 1971, 1972, 1973, 1975, 1977 by The Lockman Foundation. Used by permission. Other references are from Today's English Version; New Testament Copyright © American Bible Society 1966, 1971, 1976, and from The Living Bible, copyright 1971 by Tyndale House Publishers, Wheaton, Ill. Used by permission.

Library of Congress Cataloging-in-Publication Data

Ogilvie, Lloyd John.
    Climbing the rainbow : claiming God's promises in the storms of life / Lloyd Ogilvie.
      p. cm.
    ISBN 0–8499–0762–4
        0–8499–3523–7
    1. God—Promises—Biblical teaching.   2. Consolation—Biblical teaching.   3. Rainbow—Religious aspects—Christianity.   4. Christian life—Presbyterian authors.   I. Title.
BS680.P68045   1993
248.4'851—dc20   93–978
                                         CIP

34569 LB 987654321

Printed in the United States of America

To Doctors Edith and Robert Munger
For all they have meant to my wife, Mary Jane, and me.

Deo volente—carpe diem!

Contents

Acknowledgments

Deep appreciation is expressed to those who have helped make this book possible.

I am thankful for the creative working relationship I have enjoyed with Word Publishing for more than twenty years. As an author, I am grateful for the encouragement, vision, and assistance given to all the books I have written. I am indebted to Kip Jordon for the conversations, phone calls, and letters that helped shape the focus of this book in its initial stages. Joey Paul has been a faithful friend and adviser to me as "point person" for the development and completion of this project.

Over the years, my friend William McCalmont, my church's librarian, has assisted me in my research in preparation for preaching and writing.

My gratitude is also expressed to June Mears for typing and editing the chapters of the manuscript for submission to the publisher. Her expertise and enthusiasm for the project are deeply appreciated.

The preparation of this book was done on a summer study leave in Edinburgh, Scotland. In part, this study leave was made possible by a grant from the Bertha Urban Kinsey Memorial Fund through the California Community Foundation. The memory of Bertha and Ira Kinsey continues to inspire me as I seek to communicate the faith, hope, and love in Christ that they lived so magnificently.

Preface

Recently, while being driven from the San Francisco airport to one of the suburbs for a speaking engagement, I was delighted to see that someone had painted the many-splendored colors of a rainbow on the concrete entrance of a tunnel through which the freeway passed.

"How wonderful!" I exclaimed to my friend who was driving. "It's great to see a reminder of the covenant on a freeway."

"Sorry, Lloyd," my friend replied. "That rainbow was painted there by some self-realization group. I don't think they had the biblical covenant in mind."

"How sad," I said as we entered the tunnel. "The rainbow is one of the most powerful biblical symbols of the covenant God made with Noah and fulfilled in the new covenant in Jesus Christ."

"That may be true," my friend replied, "but if you talk about the rainbow around here, you'll be classified as one of those human-potential thinkers."

Coming out of the tunnel into the brightness of the early afternoon sun, I explained, "But the rainbow is a very illusive symbol unless it is attached to the covenant and Christ. Nature's rainbow can be its most magnificent symbol. It is also its most evanescent; it vanishes while you are still admiring it. A rainbow without Christ can symbolize little more than a vague spiritual longing."

"Well, that's about all it is to most people," my friend agreed.

I went on, "Maybe we evangelical Christians have not talked enough about the covenant faithfulness of God and now are intimidated by self-aspiration groups who have adopted the rainbow as their symbol, without the cross. Actually, when

Christ is the rainbow in our hearts, we can endure the storms of life around us. And when we feel we've failed or we begin to wonder why we have to face so many stormy days of difficulty, He's the rainbow reaching across the imagined breach we may feel."

As we drove on, my friend and I talked intently about times when we'd experienced the Lord's covenant faithfulness in the storms of our personal and professional lives and were given the assurance of Christ's rainbow in the rain.

When we reached our destination, I said, "Let's not give up the rainbow as our symbol. It's biblical and it's powerful."

My friend turned to me and said, "You ought to write a book about the true meaning of the rainbow and the Lord's willingness to bless us in the storms."

"I think I will," I said firmly. I decided that the biblical rainbow of the covenant would be the focus of my studies the following summer in Edinburgh, Scotland.

During the first week of that preparation time for writing this book, the familiar line from an old hymn, "I trace the rainbow in the rain," kept going through my mind. When I investigated the origin of those words, I discovered a little-known fact of history that started me *climbing* the rainbow. Then I knew how I wanted to begin this book. Wonder what this could be? Turn the page.

1

Climbing the Rainbow

I set My rainbow in the cloud, and it shall be for the sign of the covenant between Me and the earth. . . . that the rainbow shall be seen in the cloud.

Genesis 9:13–14

---

*I*t was late in the evening of June 6, 1882. The pastor of the church in Innellan on the Firth of Clyde in Scotland sat alone in the darkness of his study. No need to turn up the gaslights. He was blind.

Then forty years old, he had emerged as one of Scotland's most brilliant preachers and compelling poets. Crowds flooded to hear him wherever he preached; prestigious churches in Edinburgh and Glasgow sought him to be their pastor; his books and poetry were read throughout the land.

On that night in June, however, the darkness that had increasingly gathered around him since childhood was matched by a darkness in his heart. He experienced an inner anguish.

It had been a long day. In the morning he had attended the marriage service for one of his sisters. A mixture of happiness and pain surged in his heart. This sister had been his eyes all through his student days in college and seminary. She learned Latin, Greek, and Hebrew so she could read for him. With her assistance he had been a brilliant student, graduating with the highest honors the University of Glasgow had to award. She accompanied him as he began his ministry, writing out his dictated sermons and reading them back to him until they were fully memorized and could then be delivered with his impelling oratorical skill. What would he do without her?

After the wedding, the blind poet-preacher took a steamer from Glasgow to Innellan. "Something happened to me," he wrote later, "which was known only to myself, and which caused me the most severe mental suffering."

Was it facing the demands of his life and ministry without his sister's eyes? Was it that his sister's marriage forced him to realize that he would probably never marry? Or had he endured the rejection of someone he had hoped to marry? Were there fantasies too aberrant to relate stalking the corridors of his mind?

We dare not press behind the veil of his own confession, "Something happened . . . which caused me severe mental suffering." Perhaps it's a good thing we don't know the details: It leaves us to fill in the blanks with our own brand of "mental suffering"—anxiety, worry, stress, fear, rejection, loss, grief.

What we do know is that on that night the poet sought to battle through his anguish to a new and profound experience of the love and faithfulness of God.

A Cherished Image

The rainbow, the biblical sign of God's covenant, had been a cherished image of the untiring constancy of His grace. A rainbow was one of the last things the preacher-poet saw before complete blindness set in. We should not be surprised then that the image of the rainbow appeared often in his poems. The first line in one of them discloses the personal nature of the rainbow to him: "Jesus, rainbow of my sorrow." In another we have, "And all the tears are rainbow bright when Calvary crowns the way," and still another runs, "the rainbow view, the springtime of my days."

And so, with the rainbow of God's love flashing in his mind, the poet felt His presence and received the courage to go on. His anguish was overcome by God's love. He picked up his pen and wrote his most famous poem—and one of the best-loved hymns of the ages. "The hymn was the fruit of suffering. It was the quickest bit of work I ever did in my life. I had the impression rather of having it dictated by some inward Voice than of working it out myself. I am quite sure the whole work was completed in five minutes." The first and third stanzas capture what happened that night in June.

> O Love that wilt not let me go,
> I rest my weary soul in thee;
> I give thee back the life I owe,
> That in thine ocean depths its flow
> May richer, fuller be.
>
> O Joy that seekest me through pain,
> I cannot close my heart to thee;
> *I climb the rainbow through the rain,*
> And feel the promise is not vain
> That morn shall tearless be.

A Misquoted Line?

By now, many of you have realized that the preacher-poet was George Matheson, who went on to be one of the greatest preachers of the nineteenth century. And those of you who are familiar with this famous poem and hymn may think I have misquoted the third line of the third stanza.

Not so. That's how Matheson wrote it: "I climb the rainbow through the rain"! It was a prosy hymnal committee of the Church of Scotland that insisted it be changed to "I trace the rainbow through the rain." The members of the committee could not imagine anything so fanciful and farcical as climbing a rainbow!

"That will not do," they said with the criticism poets and artists often suffer from those who have not grappled with the heart-wrenching crises that often give birth to verbal images. And finally, Matheson consented to the change with regret, permitting a line he would never have written.

How sad! A close friend of Matheson, J. Morrison of Colinton, Scotland, expressed it in an article for *The Scotsman* years later. "It was no mere mundane rainbow that was envisioned, anymore than rain (sorrow) meant physical rain, for Matheson was both mystic and seer. When 'I climb the rainbow' was altered to 'I trace the rainbow,' the figure of a victorious ascent of the spirit toward its divine source (a purely inner experience) was changed to passive contemplation of an external phenomenon mentally envisaged—pious and beautiful in its way, but quite different from what was originally implied."[1]

The blind poet remembered the magnificent rainbows he had seen as a youth. They appeared in the midst of the storm while it was still raining. This brought to mind the rainbow as the sign of God's covenant with Noah and all perpetual generations. It reached from heaven to earth and spanned the skies. For Matheson, the rainbow was like Jacob's ladder let down from heaven for the poet's ascent into the glory of God.

James Black, in a book published fifty-four years after Matheson's death, wrote: "It is merely silly to think of Matheson 'tracing' that rainbow through the rain; his eyes were shut forever! But in his own fine imagination, he could picture himself stumbling forward blindly till he actually touched the rainbow with his groping fingers! And when he touched it, he could grasp it and climb it . . . God's rainbows are not to be traced, but climbed."[2]

More Than Scientific Definition

Oh, sure, we can define a rainbow with scientific precision. We know that it is an arch of light formed opposite the sun during or after the close of a storm, exhibiting the colors of the spectrum, caused by the refraction and dispersion of light in drops of water falling through the air. But no definition of the physical phenomenon of a rainbow touches the delight we feel when we see one. We say with Wordsworth, "My heart leaps up when I behold a rainbow in the sky." And Sir Walter Scott:

> What human limner e'er would choose
> To paint the rainbow's varying hues
> Unless to mortal it were given
> To dip his brush in the dyes of heaven.

It is no less true for a wordsmith. My pen must be dipped in biblical truth about rainbows in the rain. I must know what they have meant to God and His people through the span of biblical history before I can communicate what they mean to us today. As we shall discover more thoroughly in succeeding chapters, God has identified the rainbow as His sign of His covenant love, "I set My rainbow in the cloud, and it shall be for the sign of the covenant between Me and the earth. . . . that the rainbow shall be seen in the cloud" (Gen. 9:13–14).

It is little wonder then that Ezekiel described his vision of the glory of God, "Like the appearance of a rainbow . . . on a rainy day" (Ezek. 1:28). And the apostle John's vision of God's throne in heaven affirming the inseparable union of His reigning power and the reach of His grace, "And One sat on the throne. . . . and there was a rainbow around the throne, in appearance like an emerald" (Rev. 4:2–3). The rainbow of God's love spans the Scriptures.

Serendipity in Suffering

God's rainbow in the rain is a serendipity of hope in our suffering. It is not only the outstretched hand of God that reaches out to grasp our hands; much more, it is a firm passage along which He draws us into His presence. Along the way, the prism-splendors flash: the purple of His sovereignty, the crimson of the blood of the pascal lamb and the Lamb of Calvary, the blue of His faithfulness, the orange of His hope, the bright yellow of His repeated offers of new beginnings.

"I Will" Rainbow Promises

Throughout the Bible there are powerful "I will" promises. They proclaim what the Lord is ready and willing to do for us. At several crucial moments in Israel's development, God, whose primary name, Yahweh, means "I will be who I will be," appeared to reaffirm the covenant made with Noah and promised what He would do. Each of these promises tell us what He can and will do for us today.

Then in the New Testament, Christ gives fifteen "I will" promises with stunning authority. Each promise deals with one of our urgent problems.

Climbing the rainbow is claiming the promises of God! It's an active, positive choice we make; it's an activity of the will. Claiming these promises one by one, grasping their contemporary meaning, living in their assurance, and believing God is what climbing the rainbow really means.

Driving the Stake

As we claim each "I will" promise, we are like mountain climbers. Every few feet along the way, up the steep rocky pitch of the mountain, the climber drives a piton, or stake. A six-foot rope is tied to the piton and around the climber. He can then move on to the next place to drive another piton, knowing he will fall no farther than the length of the rope attached to the last piton he drove into the mountainside.

In a similar fashion, each time we claim one of the promises of the Lord, we drive a piton and then cannot fall farther than the last piton-promise we claimed as an anchor. The Christian life does not need to be one of constantly slipping and falling back to where we began in the first place.

In each chapter of this book we will drive a piton as we claim and live one or more of the promises of the willingness of the Lord. As we climb the rainbow in the rain of our needs, we will ascend to the heights of His glory and grace. We don't have to spend the rest of our lives in the valley of spiritual immaturity.

The Note of Panic

As I listen to people in deep conversations and read thousands of letters from my radio and television audiences, I hear a note of panic. The pressures of life are really getting to people today. So many do not sense a close relationship with God. Others feel He has let them down and are actually angry with Him. Lots of them are going through tough times and wonder what good can come out of what they are enduring. They find it difficult to trust the Lord.

With equal intensity, others feel they have failed Him or have not measured up to the standards they have set for themselves. Still others wonder why their faith is not more vibrant and powerful.

When we feel a distance from God, He must make the first move: He must reach across the breach, the yawning gap we feel exists between Him and us. This reach across the breach is called the covenant, God's choice to be our God, to never let us go.

In turbulent times, when the clouds of trouble cover the sky and you feel your life is socked-in for an endless storm, watch for a break in the clouds, a ray of sun, and the rainbow in the rain. And then start climbing the rainbow!

Fancy? Poetic imagery? It was more than that for George Matheson. That June night was a turning point. He discovered again that the God of the covenant would not let him go; joy reached him in his pain. He climbed the rainbow and claimed God's promise to never leave or forsake him. "I shall endeavor to forget my thorn," he said. "I shall do my work in spite of it; the mission of my life shall not fail because of physical sufferings. I shall fulfill my God-appointed task in the face of every hardship and pain."

Back to the Future

One rainy day last summer, I made a trip to the village of Innellan. It was a delight to walk down Matheson Lane and visit the church he made famous. I sat alone in one of the pews. Another one of Matheson's poems, memorized years before, sounded in my soul with new intensity.

> Make me a captive Lord
> And then I shall be free
> Force me to render up my sword
> And I shall conqueror be
> I sink in life's alarms
> When by myself I stand
> Imprison me within Thine arms
> And strong shall be my hand.
>
> My heart is weak and poor
> Until it Master find
> It has no spring of action sure
> It varies in the wind
> It cannot freely move
> Till Thou has wrought its chain

Enslave me with Thy matchless love
And deathless it shall reign.

My will is not my own
Till Thou hast made it Thine
If I should reach a monarch's throne
It must its throne resign
It only stand unbent
Amidst the clashing strife
When on Thy bosom it has lent
And found in Thee its life.

As I drove out of the village, the rain began to let up. You guessed it. A rainbow spanned the Firth of Clyde and one end reached the village! I was deeply moved and made a fresh commitment to climb the rainbow in the rain. What I have discovered in that adventure is what I want to share in this book.

2

The Reach Across the Breach

I will remember My covenant which is between Me and you.

Genesis 9:15

We'd be shocked if a person stood up in church service and said, "Pardon me for interrupting, but I have an emergency. I'm losing my relationship with God. Will someone help me?"

Our astonishment would increase if someone else followed that by saying, "Well, as long as we're being honest, I have to say that I'm suffering a sense of distance from God. A lack of intimacy and closeness. When I became a Christian I experienced joy, but for years now I haven't sensed the Lord's presence in my prayers. Discipleship is a dutiful drudgery for me, and pretending to know God is getting more difficult all the time."

And we'd probably be very unsettled if a third person spoke up and said, "All this honesty has made me wonder if *I* know God. If I do, why am I so unsure of His love, why don't I feel forgiven, and why am I constantly thrashing about saying I need to know the will of God?"

But the final person to speak would most certainly rattle our "quilted cage." "Yes, I also wonder if I know God. If I do, why am I so often passively resistant to living what I believe? Why is my faith not more radiant and alive?"

A time of honest, open sharing of these needs would be traumatic, but very revealing. I am convinced that there are people inside and outside the church like all of these. People who need God but do not sense a deep, intimate relationship. Often this is caused by a breach.

The Breach

Allow me to explain what I mean by a breach. It is a break in a relationship, a gap in communication, a rupture of trust, an infraction of expectation. A breach happens when we think a person has not measured up to our expectations or when we feel guilty for not meeting what we thought was expected of us. A feeling of estrangement results.

Sometime ago, I felt totally misunderstood and misused by a friend. I was angry and deeply hurt. I foolishly thought I could handle it without confronting my friend. Magnaminously, I said it didn't matter, that I would forget it. Yet, as the weeks went by, there never seemed to be enough time to call him or get together. One day I realized that I no longer felt close to him; we had drifted apart. A tiff grew into a rift, then a drift, and finally a breach.

The same sense of estrangement happens when we think we have failed in a relationship. We feel guilty, defensive, or unworthy. If the failure is not brought out into the open and healed through honest confession and forgiveness, we settle for a surface relationship, avoid deep conversation, and eventually drift apart. What's worse, sometimes we find some fault in the person we've hurt and blame him or her for the breakdown of the relationship!

A Breach with God

The same dynamics can occur in our relationship with God. We may wake up some morning and feel that He seems distant; our prayers sound like a monologue and our problems look insurmountable. At first we shuck it off, blaming a bad night's rest or something we ate. When the condition persists for weeks or even months, a terrible, low-burning panic sets in. There's a breach in our relationship with God.

Often, this sense of estrangement is caused by something we've done for which we have not sought forgiveness and reconciliation with God. Life presses on. We think we've forgotten, but we haven't. Even if we push it down into our subconscious, it's still there in the computer of hidden memories, creating a conscious sense of separation from God.

For Example

My friend, Dick, is a good example. He's a leader in his church and a successful contractor. While having lunch together, he confided to me that his faith had become cold and sterile. He seldom prayed, and when he did, he felt like he was talking but no one was listening.

Dick was startled when I asked him where in his life he thought he had failed God. A stunned look appeared on his face. "There's no question about that," he said. "I really feel like a failure with one of my sons. I did pretty well with my other three children, but I've really messed up with this kid."

I tried to help Dick see that his sense of unresolved failure was creating a feeling of unworthiness with God. Certainly the failure with his boy was not imagined; he *had* neglected this particular child in his family. So as he grew up, the boy used all the wrong means of getting his father's attention. He was an under-achiever in school, got into drugs, and developed a lifestyle abhorrent to his father.

At a time when Dick needed God's help the most, he felt he could not go to Him—that's the terrible result of a breach. But now Dick had to play the ball where it was on the field. He could not redo the past, but he could ask for the Lord's forgiveness.

When he did, he was set free to seek guidance from the Lord on how to rebuild his relationship with his son. That required the openness to admit to his son what he perceived to be his failure in the relationship over the years. Most important of all, he changed his attitude toward his son, made time to be with him, and made a long-term commitment of communicating how much he loved him.

"How's it going?" I asked Dick some months later. "It's going to take a long time," Dick said honestly, "but I'm not alone in the battle. I feel the closeness with God I thought I had lost."

Unconfessed Failure

A television actress, whom I will call Sally, once paid a high price for an acting job: a sexual relationship with a director. It brought her the success in her career that she craved, but diminished her sense of the presence of God in her life.

Sally told no one and pressed on with her busy life in the Hollywood industry. Though she had been an active Christian since her teens, in her words "born-again, filled with the Spirit, evangelical and all," she noticed that her joy in her faith began to wane. She felt an inner uneasiness around other Christians, her daily devotions became sporadic, and she complained about the problem of unanswered prayer. God had not changed, but she had. A breach with God caused the drift from God.

What startled me was that the affair with the director had happened fifteen years before she came to see me about her problem with unanswered prayer. She took a long time beating around that theological bush before I had an opportunity to say, "Sometimes our problems with prayer grow out of an estrangement with God." Finally, she blurted out what had happened years before. Healing could not take place until the breach was faced, forgiven, and, by grace, really forgotten.

An Accumulated Breach

Often, the breach is not as clearly defined as Dick's or Sally's. Sometimes, it's an accumulation of lots of little failures. We all have an inner list of dicta, rules, regulations, and obligations that we've been taught are crucial to keeping a strong relationship with God. When we pile up a bunch of shortcomings—failures to do and be what we think God expects—there's a moment in time when we judge ourselves as unworthy of His presence, love, guidance, and strength. A breach develops because of our attitudes about ourselves. We don't feel we have a right to a relationship with God because of our lack of follow-through on what's required.

The Breach of Judging God

Now we come to the really big breach—stay with me here, this may be more of a problem than you might think at first. Equally debilitating is a breach with God caused by our judgment of *Him.*

Life, for most people, has not worked out the way they planned. Many have been through disappointments and discouragements. Some have experienced physical illness and handicaps. Still others have lost loved ones, and the grief has been almost unbearable. We've all had our share of physical, emotional, and relational problems. Tough, even tragic, things do happen. Sometimes we feel like we are a moving target for trouble.

At the same time, we try to hang on to our belief in the goodness and faithfulness of God. To do that, we blame the bad things that happen on the thoughtlessness, carelessness, or just plain cussedness of people.

So far, so good. But then, as we experience tragedies in our lives and witness them in others, often there is no other explanation for

31

CLIMBING THE RAINBOW

them except that some are due to a massive evil at work in the world, or that they occur because of the diabolical mischief of Satan himself. So, even with that acknowledgment, we can keep our faith strong and firm in God's providence.

But when life dishes out what seems to be unfair or prolonged suffering, we begin to wonder, "Where is God in all of this? If He is sovereign of all, and nothing happens without His knowledge and permission, why (yes, why?) does He allow, not only the clouds, but the vicious storms that go with them?"

Because we have not done some sound thinking about suffering—about how God can use it and how we must trust Him even when we can't see any possible good resulting from bad things that happen—we get disappointed with God. Sometimes we are downright angry at what He has allowed to happen. Our sense of justice, which is actually part of our inheritance from God, is turned against Him! When we need Him most, He becomes our enemy. A breach happens in our hearts and God is the cause . . . or so we think.

Oh, most of us never openly admit *this* breach. But our questions linger. Our trust is weakened. Soon we complain that our relationship with God is simply not as joyous or powerful or meaningful as before. Very often we can't pray.

A Tragic Accident

A couple lost their seventeen-year-old son in a tragic auto accident. They had prayed daily for, and with, their son. They claimed God's promise to protect believers' children. And yet, late one night a truck that was illegally parked on a lane of the freeway suddenly loomed up before their son's car. He couldn't turn quickly enough to avoid it. The impact killed him; the flames that exploded around him charred his body.

Two years after his death, both parents still battled grief. Their son had been outstanding: a committed Christian and a leader in his school. Also a talented young composer, he had written a song entitled "Dancing in Paradise." The paradise he wrote about was the sheer joy of living here as a Christian; as he wrote it, he did not know that in a few months he would be in the eternal paradise.

There has never been any question about the fact that the young man is alive with God. This faith of his parents has sustained them through the pain of grief. However, when I did a survey of the needs of our congregation and asked people to share with me the promise they needed most to claim, the mother wrote a long letter in response. "Lloyd," she said, "it's difficult to claim another promise when we really prayed and believed the promise that God would protect our son. I guess I'm angry at God."

Who could not empathize with that? And yet, more than empathy was required. The parents continued to worship and pray. They reaffirmed their conviction that death was not an ending for their son. He is alive with the God he loved so deeply during his short life. Was quantity of years better than quality? Would they have wanted him with them for seventy years as an unbeliever?

Over the months they battled to maintain their faith and to receive God's healing. He had not caused the accident. He has permitted us to live in a free world in which tragedies can happen: They are often simply the distressing, heartbreaking result of human actions and choices—ours, and those of others. God, too, suffers with us.

Finally, the parents allowed God to heal their grief and terrible loneliness for their son. When they did, they were set free, and the healing continues. Because they could admit they were angry at God, recognize the breach, and seek His help, they are finding new peace and courage.

But what about all the people who have never admitted to a breach in their relationship with God? Not only the ones with scar tissue layered over a gigantic grief, but all the others who are inwardly angry over how things have worked out for them?

The idea that we might be angry with God is scary, so we suppress it. We just don't feel close to Him, and what seems on the surface to be merely benign neglect of our relationship with God is often a camouflage for passive *resistance*. And what do we do with the anger? We turn it on ourselves and try to hurt God by hurting ourselves!

The Pain and the Panic

Whether our drift from God began with a failure of ours or our disagreement with Him about how He's managed things, it makes little difference in the final analysis. Either way, we still feel the terrible pain of separation from Him and the panic of having to carry the burden of life alone. Is panic too strong a word? I don't think so. It aptly describes the anxiety and stress we feel each time a new crisis hits.

Norman Cousins called panic the ultimate enemy; I say it is the sharpest tool of the ultimate enemy: Satan. Panic keeps us on Red Alert. We live in a crisis mode. Our nervous systems are filled with agitation. And we really are in trouble whenever we conclude that things are the way they will always have to be! Our anger with God becomes a breach when we refuse to admit the estrangement and won't allow Him to help us.

The Reach Across the Breach

At a time like that, we need the God of the covenant to reach across the breach. He will not leave us in our morass of guilt or self-pity, our anger, or our questioning of His providence. He has chosen to be our God and elected us to be His people, and He has made powerful promises of what He will do to help us. The first of the "I will" promises we will claim and climb deals directly with what He will do when we feel a breach between Him and us. It is the basic promise that describes the way God has chosen to deal with His people. In fact, it is *a promise to keep a promise.* It is the very essence of the azure assurance of the rainbow.

In our time, when the symbol of the rainbow has been separated from its biblical roots, it's crucial to clarify its true meaning. What we need to rediscover is what God is thinking about when He sends a rainbow as His reach across the breach. This "I will" promise we need to grasp, grip, claim, and climb is awesome: "I will remember My covenant which is between Me and you" (Gen. 9:15).

Good News to Noah and to Us

This "I will" promise was good news for Noah, who had bobbed about in the ark for 150 days during the flood. It's even better news to us as we read it through the dilated lens of Calvary. Actually, the promise encompasses what happened thousands of years later on the cross. Let's consider what this promise meant to Noah, to God Himself, and then to us when we experience the panic of what feels like a breach between God and us.

During the long days and nights in the ark, Noah contemplated the nature of his God. He had witnessed the fierce judgment and wrath of God against rebellious, sinful humankind. The people God had created to know, love, and glorify Him sought to be gods themselves—gods over their own lives and the resources of the natural world He had entrusted to them to enjoy. The judgment of the flood had resulted.

Noah must have shuddered as he thought about the future. He and his kin were the sole survivors of humankind. God had promised a new beginning for His creation. But would there be repeated judgment, like the flood? Was violent wrath God's only way of dealing with sin? Talk about a breach! Noah felt it intensely. How could he ever fulfill the demands of his fierce and righteous God?

When the flood subsided and the ark landed on dry ground, Noah and his kin were happy to leave the constricted confines of what had been their lifeboat. We can only imagine the surging delight Noah felt when he looked up and saw the sun piercing through an opening in the clouds. Then he saw the breathtaking sight: across the sky was the azure magnificence of a rainbow!

As Noah stood there, stunned by the splendor, God spoke to him. What He said gave meaning to the rainbow that Noah would never forget. And we must not miss the meaning if we are going to see spiritual rainbows in the rain with the eyes of our hearts.

With Noah, we must discover that there is more than wrath in the heart of God. There is rainbow mercy!

> Thus I establish My covenant with you: Never again shall all flesh be cut off by the waters of the flood; never again shall there be a flood to destroy the earth. . . . This is the sign of the covenant which I make between Me and you, and every living creature that is with you, for perpetual generations. I set My rainbow in the cloud, and it shall be for the sign of the covenant between Me and the earth. It shall be, when I bring a cloud over the earth, that the rainbow shall be seen in the cloud; *and I will remember My covenant which is between Me and you.* . . . the rainbow shall be in the cloud, and I will look on it to remember the everlasting covenant.
>
> Genesis 9:11–16, italics added

God's Plan

There you have it: a direct, penetrating statement of how God plans to manage His fallen creation. He will not deny the freedom of will He has given to humankind; He will never again, until the end of history, destroy the earth in judgment. God's mercy will outdistance His wrath. He will bear with His sinful people, suffer with them and for them. He will even bring good out of the evil that people do while exercising their freedom of choice. The problems they bring on themselves and inflict on others will never go beyond the reach of His transforming power. He will pursue and woo His children constantly, seeking to help them exercise their freedom of will in choosing to glorify and obey Him out of love. He will send leaders, prophets, and kings to lead His people.

Finally, in the fullness of time, God will send His own Son to suffer for the sins of the world. All of this is in the eleven words of His rainbow-splendored promise, "I will remember My covenant which is between Me and you."

God's Covenant

The word "covenant" here means an irrevocable bond. God has pledged Himself to how He will deal with us. He will not forget us or the promise He has made to be merciful, gracious, and kind.

But What About the Clouds?

Whether we read the words of God to Noah literally or figuratively, we end up with the same question: Why the clouds? We must be as clear about the meaning of the clouds as we are about the rainbow!

The clouds represent the dark times that God permits while we come to grips with what is happening to us. We cannot deny God's blunt statement that there will be clouds and He will send them: "When I bring a cloud over the earth."

It's during the cloudy, stormy times that we hear life's most abhorred word. It's more challenging than a "yes" that spells a go-ahead for some longed for but sinew-stretching opportunity; it's more frustrating than a definite "no" that lowers a death blow to a cherished dream. This word is disliked by youth, the least welcome word all through our lives, the dreaded word of the visionary, the resisted word when we want results in ourselves or other people *now,* and the distressing word for the sick or those who love them. This word is one we'd like to extricate from our lexicons forever. The word I'm talking about is *wait.*

Sara Doudney was right:

> There are days of silent sorrow
> In the seasons of our life;
> There are wild despairing moments,
> There are hours of mental strife;
> There are times of stony anguish,
> When the tears refuse to fall;
> But the waiting time, my brothers,
> Is the hardest time of all. . . .
>
> We can bear the heat of conflict,
> Though the sudden, crushing blow,
> Beating back our gathered forces,
> For a moment lay us low;
> We may rise again beneath it
> None the weaker for the fall;
> But the waiting time, my brothers,
> Is the hardest time of all.[1]

Airports, train stations, and hospitals are not exclusive in having waiting rooms. Sometimes it seems like a lot of life is one large waiting room, an anteroom of expectation for some fulfilling and satisfying experience. And while we wait, we tire of the trite reminder: "All things come to those who wait." We much prefer Thomas Edison's philosophy: "Everything comes to him who hustles while he waits." But what if we're unsure of what to hustle or if previous hustling has not worked out for the best?

We turn to the Bible in those cloudy, stormy waiting times. And guess what? From psalmist, prophet, and apostle comes the same distressing word: *wait!* But this word is compacted in a power-packed phrase: *Wait on the Lord.* That's the answer David got when he presented his lament to the Lord: "Wait on the LORD; / Be of good courage, / And He shall strengthen your heart; / Wait, I say, on the LORD!" (Ps. 27:14). Isaiah was even more specific about what waiting in God can do for us. "Those who wait on the LORD / Shall renew their strength; / They shall mount up with wings like eagles, / They shall run and not be weary, / They shall walk and not faint" (Isa. 40:31).

It's so important that we understand what waiting on God is *not* before we can grasp what it really means. Waiting on God sometimes conjures up a picture of a tired-out, elderly deity who is lagging behind our forward movement, trying to catch up with us. There's a touch of arrogance in the confession, "I must have been running ahead of God." Ahead of God? The omnipresent God is always ahead of us, for He is the Lord of the present and the future. We *can* run away from Him or fill our lives so full there's no time to listen to Him. Sometimes the cloudy, stormy times force us to stop in our mad race toward our self-fashioned goals.

The other thing waiting on God is *not* is cajoling God to come to us. Waiting on God is to condition us to receive Him. He is already present. *God Himself is the answer* to our deepest needs and most urgent questions. So waiting on God is not pas-sive, but active. It's responding to His call to communion with Him. "Before they call, I will answer; / And while they are still speaking, I will hear" (Isa. 65:24). Waiting on God is reporting in for a renewed relationship with God, who has been waiting for us to realize how much we need Him. Abiding in Him is what wait-ing on God really means.

Two magnificent gifts are provided as we wait on, abide in, God. The first is patience. Don't pray for patience; God may have to give you situations in which you are forced to learn it. Rather, wait on God. It is in His presence that we discover His timing and His will. Sometimes the result of waiting on God is a creative im-patience with what He reveals that needs to be changed in us, our relationships, or the world around us. Divine discontent often leads to our most decisive changes.

But not without the second gift of waiting on God: power. The supernatural strength of the Holy Spirit is given for what God clarifies is to be done. It's simply impossible to "Be of good cour-age" without the coupled blessing, "He will strengthen your heart." While we wait on God, abiding in His presence, listening for His guidance, He conditions us with His wisdom and discern-ment.

Just this last week, I awoke one day with my mind and heart clouded over with thunderclouds of problems and perplexities. Inside, every part of my being was spinning with solutions I had worked out. I raced through my morning devotions of adoration, confession, supplication, intercession, and dedication. What I left out, in my impetuous mood, was silence. At the end of a half hour, I was no more ready for the day than when I started. Even though I longed to get on with the day of working out my own plans, I knew it was perilous to try. The Lord seemed to be saying, "Start all over again. Go back through the steps of prayer and don't forget silence. Wait on Me!"

In an unhurried way, I began with praise, lingering to love and enjoy the Lord. I confessed my anxiety and worry, felt the assurance of His forgiveness, then spread out before Him not my solutions for His help, but His solutions for which He promised power.

As I think back on that day, I am alarmed by what might have happened if I had insisted on my plans. What the Lord gave me to say and do as I waited on Him was not only superior to what I had worked out myself, but it brought results I could never have produced on my own. At the end of the day, I was more than ready to say with the psalmist, "My soul, wait silently for God alone, / For my expectation is from Him. / He only is my rock and salvation; / He is my defense; / I shall not be moved. / In God is my salvation and my glory; / The rock of my strength, / And my refuge, is in God" (Ps. 62:5–7).

The mystics talk about the cloud of unknowing and the dark night of the soul that can happen at high noon. It is during these cloudy, dark times that we see ourselves as we are and admit how desperately we need God. We struggle with the mind-stretching truth that God made His most painful choice when He gave us free will, knowing full well how we would misuse our freedom.

It's when the sky of life is covered with clouds that we do our hard thinking about what we have done with our freedom: what we've done to ourselves and to others. It's the time when we get in touch with our need for forgiveness. It's also the time when we identify the hurts and wrongs that others have done to us; then we are confronted with how difficult it is to really forgive.

While the clouds still hang heavy, we wrestle with the realization that life very often isn't fair. How could it be, in a deranged world where so few play by God's rules of righteousness and justice? But then we must question our own shallow understanding of fairness: a happy, easy, problem-free, successful life? Isn't prosperity our divine right? Not if we consider the women and men of the Bible and Christian history! Some of the greatest of them endured inexplicable suffering and knew God more intimately because of it than those who indemnified God to produce what they wanted, when they wanted it.

The clouds will cover the sky until we can identify our own suffering. Sometimes it's physical pain; other times, guilt or grief; still other times, emotional hurts, lurking memories, worry over others, anxiety about the future.

Frankly, I have known cloudy periods that have included all of the above thoughts and feelings. But over the years, I have discovered a liberating truth: They don't have to last for a prolonged time. When storm clouds bring me to a realization of how much I need God, I cry out to Him, telling Him that more than anything or anyone else I long for Him to reach across my imagined breach and tell me what He will do to give me a fresh start. Then I hear His whisper in my soul, "I will remember My covenant which is between Me and you."

The clouds of doubt, fear, and anxiety break; the sun shines through again. Sometimes God actually produces a rainbow in the sky, but most often it's a rainbow in my heart. Then I know that He has reached across the breach.

But let me be very honest: It's not all blue skies afterward. The clouds don't vanish immediately. The storm, though, is over. The heavy black clouds that once blocked the sun slowly begin to disappear, sprinkling their last little showers. Now we know that good things are coming. And remember, it's the final raindrops after the storm that serve the sun in producing the rainbow!

William Cowper was right:

You fearful saints, fresh courage take
The clouds you so much dread
Are filled with mercy and shall break
With blessings on your head.

3

God Is Cookin' Up a Rainbow

And Abraham called the name of the place, The-Lord-Will-Provide. . . ."By Myself I have sworn, says the Lord, because you have done this thing, and have not withheld your son, your only son—in blessing I will bless you."

Genesis 22:14, 16–17

A little boy in Missouri loved to watch with his dad the magnificent display of nature in an Ozark rainstorm. One day when the boy saw a storm approaching, he ran to get his dad to enjoy the awesome moment together. His dad, a Church of the Nazarene pastor, set aside his work to join his son on the porch. The lad took his dad by the hand and led him outside.

Hand in hand they watched the approaching storm as it swept across the tree-covered Ozark mountains of Southern Missouri. They beheld the lightning, heard the thunder, and felt the spray from the earth-replenishing rain. After the rain subsided, a refreshing breeze filled them with the delicious smells of wet grass and grain as well as the perfume from the trees and flowers.

While the clouds still hung dense in the sky, the little boy squeezed his dad's hand. As the boy relished the delectable aromas he said, "Dad, I think I smell a rainbow cookin'!"

God is constantly cooking up rainbows. They are reassurances of His faithfulness of His covenant with us. Remember that His covenant is His choice to be our God and His call to us to be His people. But there are times when our trust in His faithfulness is sorely tested by the circumstances of life. Too often, our lives are filled with the thunderclouds of doubt. Sometimes we even think He's wrong and we're right about what's best for us. When we rush off, following our idea of what's best, our inner storm reaches its peak: We wonder if God has forgotten about us.

It's through these clouds God sends His rainbows to us. These rainbows tell us He is ready to begin again with us. They come as reaffirmations of what He will do for us, articulated in strong "I will" promises expressing His determination to work out His will in our lives.

The Old Testament is filled with God's interventions in the lives of His chosen, covenant people during which He spoke these "I will" promises. From the hundreds of these "I will" assurances I want to select just a few. We will note the ones that are most personally applicable for us to use as pitons to climb the rainbow of the covenant. We will claim the promises given to Abraham and Jacob and then the greatest one given to Moses. Then we will press on, climbing the rainbow of the covenant with promises given through the prophets. All the Old Testament "I will" promises we'll consider are to remind us of the solid biblical truth: God never forgets us and His rainbows in the rain are on time when we doubt His providence and need to learn again to do things His way.

The Lord Will Provide

Abraham towers as a man of faith in God's covenant faithfulness. Yahweh called Abraham to be the father of succeeding generations of His people. Most of all, God called Abraham to be His friend. Subsequent Scripture affirms this friendship: "Abraham, Your friend forever" (2 Chron. 20:7). And God's own words through Isaiah, "Abraham My friend" (Isa. 41:8). This friendship allowed Abraham to know God by one of His greatest names *YHWH-YIREH*, meaning, "the Lord will provide."

Long before Abraham came to know God by this name, he received an awesome promise that would eventually bring him to a traumatic personal experience of the name's meanings. When Abraham left Ur in Northern Mesopotamia, the Lord said to him,

> Go forth from your country,
> And from your relatives
> And from your father's house,
> To the land which I will show you.
> And I will make you a great nation,
> And I will bless you,
> And make your name great;
> And so you shall be a blessing;
> And I will bless those who bless you,
> And the one who curses you I will curse.
> And in you all the families of the earth shall be
>   blessed.
>
> Genesis 12:1–3 NASB

During the long years of Abraham's life, his friendship with God grew. Yet this friendship became strained as he and his wife Sara waited for a son through whom Abraham could receive the promise of being the father of a great nation. How could he be the father of multitudes without a son? Then when Abraham was a hundred years old and Sara was ninety, the Lord made Abraham another promise: He and Sara would have a son! Both Abraham and Sara laughed at God's humanly impossible promise. Appropriately, when their son was born, they named him Isaac, which means "laughter." Abraham and Sara laughed at God over the impossibility; when God pulled off the miracle, they laughed with Him in sheer joy.

Isaac became not only Abraham's joy but also his pride. And, like many parents since, he occasionally forgot that Isaac was a miracle of grace, God's gift.

Over the years, Abraham had slowly come to know Yahweh as One who was faithful to His promises. Abraham was thankful Yahweh was not like Molech, the god of the nomadic people who appeased their god with child sacrifices.

So we can appreciate why Abraham was shocked beyond comprehension when Yahweh told him to go to Mount Moriah and make a sacrifice of Isaac. Reading the account of this incredulous command in Genesis 22, we are astounded that Abraham complied. The only possible explanation is that Abraham had learned through years of experience that Yahweh's interventions always saved him from disaster.

With complete trust that God knew what He was doing, Abraham took Isaac to the mountains. Carrying the wood for the fire for a burnt offering, a torch and a knife, Abraham trudged up the mount. Isaac followed along with understandable wonderment. And then panic. "My father!" Isaac exclaimed. "Look, the fire and the wood, but where is the lamb for the burnt offering?"

Hear the pathos mingled with strained trust in Abraham's response, "My son, God will provide for Himself the lamb for a burnt offering." Abraham's belief that God somehow would intervene was stretched to the breaking point. When Abraham arrived at the place God designated, he built an altar, placed the wood, bound Isaac, and laid him on the altar. See the look of frenzied fear in Isaac's eyes and the anguish on Abraham's tear-stained face.

At the very moment Abraham raised the knife to slay his son Isaac, the Lord called to him through an angel, "Abraham! Abraham!" With inexplicable relief, Abraham responded, "Here I am." The intervention Abraham hoped for came! "Do not lay your hand on the lad, or do anything to him; for now I know that you fear God, since you have not withheld your son, your only son, from Me," the Lord commended.

Then suddenly Abraham's transfixed attention was broken by a sound behind him. There, with its horn caught in a thicket, was a ram. Abraham knew it was the Lord's provision for the sacrifice instead of his beloved son Isaac.

I often reflect on Rembrandt's painting of this traumatic intervention of the Lord. As the great artist depicts it, just as Abraham is about to thrust the knife he looks up in response to God's intercepting call. The knife is actually flying out of his hand into the air as if he has been waiting for that Voice.

Rembrandt captures the mixture of awe, amazement, and relief on Abraham's face. The painting is more poignant when we realize that the same model for Abraham's face was also used for the father in Rembrandt's painting of the return of the prodigal son. Amazing. But should it be? Both Abraham in this instance and the father of Jesus' parable reflect the Father-heart of God.

Not surprisingly, Abraham called the mount, "The LORD will provide." The words became a cherished mnemonic name for God. "*YHWH-YIREH,* as it is said to this day," the author of Genesis comments, "in the Mount of the LORD it shall be provided." And indeed it was.

Centuries later Jerusalem was built on the hills of Moriah and the Temple was constructed by Solomon on Mount Moriah. Today, the Dome of the Rock in modern Jerusalem is built over the place where the Temple once stood. And nearby is another mount, called Golgotha.

We can fully appreciate God's "I will" promise to Abraham in Genesis 22:16 with this geographical and historical insight. "By Myself I have sworn, says the LORD, because you have done this thing, and have not withheld your son, your only son—in blessing I will bless you." God is able to bless those who love Him more than anyone. And then we discover with amazement what Abraham discovered.

Abraham realized that God loved Isaac even more than Abraham did. God didn't want the sacrifice of Isaac, but Abraham's total commitment. Yet, what God did not require of Abraham, He did require of Himself. He gave His only Son. Anything we receive in addition to this blessing is secondary. It's when secondary blessings become the primary source of our security and purpose in life that sooner or later we go through a storm caused by our distorted priorities. These secondary blessings become our Isaacs.

Who or What Is My Isaac?

The Isaac of our life can be a person: a mate, a child, a cherished friend. Our Isaac also can be whomever or whatever entrusted to us begins to compete with God for first place in our hearts. Who or what commands the attention of most of our waking moments (or our restless sleep) is a potential Isaac. And all of us are capable of several Isaacs. They can become idols of our hearts.

There are few storms in our lives more upsetting than the ones caused by worry or anxiety over our Isaacs. Whatever threatens our Isaacs causes lightning and thunder in our hearts. We become defensively territorial when we forget that they are gifts of God to us.

And yet God wants us to know that He loves our Isaacs more than we do. He cares profoundly for the people in our lives and the concerns that come to mean so much to us. All He asks is that we worship Him and not them. He also asks us to surrender our anxieties about them. It's in our Isaac-crises that we endure some of the greatest storms of life and are brought to complete trust in *YHWH-YIREH*, the Lord who will provide. And He does. The interventions of God are often followed by our renewed commitment to Him. We are forced to let go of our Isaacs. When we do the Lord steps in to bless the people and projects we clutched so tenaciously. A rainbow appears in the clouds and we hear God say, "Because you have not withheld your Isaacs, I will bless you . . . and them!"

One Step at a Time

God also cooks up a rainbow while it's still raining and we can't see the long-range purpose of His direction. Abraham's grandson, Jacob, struggled with this, even after a powerful "I will" promise was given to him—"I am God, the God of your father; do not fear to go down to Egypt, for I will make of you a great nation there. I will go down with you to Egypt, and I will also surely bring you up again" (Gen. 46:3–4).

First, some background will help us understand the meaning of this promise to Jacob and its implications for us. Jacob had twelve sons, with Joseph as his favorite. Out of competitive jealousy, Joseph's brothers sold him to a band of Ishmaelites and then told Jacob that Joseph was devoured by a wild beast. The Ishmaelites subsequently sold Joseph to Potiphar, the captain of the guard of the Pharaoh of Egypt. Significantly, the account of Joseph's life is punctuated by the oft-repeated phrase, "The Lord was with Joseph."

Good thing, because Joseph faced temptations, trials, and imprisonment. He resisted the sexual advances of Potiphar's wife for the best of reasons: "How then can I do this great wickedness, and sin against God?" (Gen. 39:9). When the woman's scheme to entice Joseph did not succeed, she accused him of doing what he had refused to do. Consequently, Joseph was placed in prison with other prisoners of the Pharaoh. Still the Lord was with Joseph.

While in prison Joseph interpreted a dream of the Pharaoh's cupbearer. After the servant was released and returned to serve the Pharaoh, he was in a strategic position to remember Joseph when the ruler had a dream that needed to be interpreted. The cupbearer told the Pharaoh about Joseph's power of interpretation of dreams. He was released from prison to make sense of the Pharaoh's dream of the seven fat and seven lean cows and the seven full and healthy heads of grain and seven thin heads of grain that devoured the good heads. Joseph gave God credit as he interpreted the dream: Egypt and surrounding territories would experience seven prosperous years followed by seven lean years; the secret of survival would be to prepare for the lean years during the seven prosperous ones.

Recognizing Joseph's divinely inspired gifts and leadership, the Pharaoh made him vice-regent over all of Egypt. The Lord was with Joseph during the seven prosperous years of preparation for the seven lean years. So effective was this preparation that Egypt was able to survive the seven lean years of famine and have an extra abundance for people from the land of Canaan who came to buy grain from them. And one delegation from Canaan was Joseph's brothers.

After a carefully staged intrigue with his brothers, Joseph finally revealed to them that he was the brother whom they had sold into slavery. "I am Joseph your brother, whom you sold into Egypt. But now, do not therefore be grieved or angry with yourselves because you sold me here; for God sent me here to preserve life. . . . It was not you who sent me here, but God" (Gen. 45:4–5, 8). With this gracious offer of forgiveness, Joseph sent his brothers back to get his father Jacob.

It was during this journey to Egypt that God gave Jacob the heartening "I will" promise of His future plans for His people. Jacob claimed this promise, not knowing how God would work it all out. His reunion with his son Joseph in Egypt is one of the most touching, heartrending scenes in the Old Testament. But what Joseph said to his brothers when they were settled in

Egypt, and after Jacob's death, has echoed down through the ages: "But as for you, you meant evil against me; but God meant it for good, in order to bring it about as it is this day, to save many people alive" (Gen. 50:20).

These words have been quoted and claimed across the centuries as people have found the secret of forgiving others who hurt or harmed them. Joseph learned the secret in retrospect; his discovery gives us a liberating perspective on what may seem like a reversal in the days ahead. "What happens—people, circumstances—may look like they have come for evil, but God *will* use them for good."

When God gives us a rainbow promise in the midst of cloudy indecision, showing us a step we are to take, it is difficult for us to respond unless we know He can use the worst that may happen— and use it for His good.

Is this stanza by an anonymous author right?

> Not till the loom is silent
> And the shuttle ceases to fly
> Will God unroll the canvas
> And explain the reason why.

Lovely poetry, but do we have to wait that long? No, the answer to the "why?" question is not in a detailed explanation from God to justify to us His ways, but in our expectations that He will work out His purposes through whatever happens at the very time we may think He's wrong. He's working with people and situations and arranging circumstances for His good for us. The only way to live with peace and serenity is to give up the assumed right to judge God, and instead to trust him. When we resign from the bogus position of trying to run our little world, we can smell that God is cooking up a rainbow in the rain.

God's Short and Long Range Plans

We saw how God maneuvered His people into Egypt for the immediate purpose of preserving the life of the sons of Jacob and their kin. But God had some long-range plans too. After they lived several years of relative privilege as the honored guests of Joseph and the Pharaoh, Joseph died and a succession of Pharaohs reigned who did not remember Joseph.

The Egyptians made the Hebrews their slaves. For more than four hundred years of servitude, the tribes named after the twelve sons of Jacob grew until the Hebrew people numbered in the hundreds of thousands. Fearing that the Hebrew slaves would revolt or side with an enemy nation and overthrow them, the Egyptians tried every method of constraining the Hebrews, including ordering the midwives to kill every male child who was born. One who escaped was a child born to a couple of the tribe of Levi.

The account of how this child was kept hidden for three months is filled with gripping drama. When keeping him hidden became too dangerous, the Lord gave his mother a plan to save him. She built a small ark of bulrushes, sealed it with asphalt and pitch, put the child in it, and floated it in the reeds of the Nile River at the exact place where she knew the Pharaoh's daughter came to bathe. The baby boy's sister was stationed to guard him.

The Pharaoh's daughter did discover the child. She realized he was a Hebrew child. Compassion filled her heart. She wanted him to be her own, but who would nurse the child? The baby's sister was ready to carry out the prearranged plan. She volunteered to find a woman to do it. And guess who she found to nurse the child! Jachabed, the real mother. She was called to nurse and raise the child in the Pharaoh's palace. The child was named Moses!

When We Think God Has Forgotten

Even while the Hebrew people thought God had forgotten them or did not care about their plight, He was working out His plan. He saved the future liberator of His people. To train Moses in His ways, God provided Moses' own mother. And to school him in military and political leadership, He placed Moses in the Pharaoh's court. As the Pharaoh's supposed grandson, Moses was in line to be the future ruler of Egypt.

But God had other plans. When Moses was forty years old, he realized he was a Hebrew and not an Egyptian. He became burdened by the suffering of his people. (Jachabed's training paid off!) But Moses took things into his own hands one day and killed a cruel Egyptian overlord who was beating a Hebrew slave. There was nothing for Moses to do but flee to the Midian desert. God used this turn of events to get His appointed leader alone so that God could reveal His name, power, and plans to Moses. At the very time the Hebrews thought their prayers were in vain, God was cooking up a rainbow, getting ready for His big move.

Near the end of Moses' forty (!) years in the desert tending sheep in the region of Mount Horeb, the Lord completed His plans for the Exodus. The long days and nights of the many years in the desert convinced Moses that he didn't know God very well. He needed to meet God and have a decisive encounter with Him.

One day, while Moses was tending his flocks on the western side of Mount Horeb, his needed encounter happened. Moses came upon a flaming acacia bush that was not consumed by the fire. Moses stood transfixed by this startling sight. And then a voice spoke out of the bush, commanding and undeniable. "Moses! Moses!" the Lord called. And Moses, who had a speech impediment, stuttered back, "Here I am."

Then the Lord revealed His true nature to Moses. He was the God of Abraham, Isaac, and Jacob. He had not forgotten His people and was ready to deliver them from Egypt. Moses was to be His leader of the deliverance. No wonder Moses stuttered out his amazement, "How? How?" He knew the military might of the Pharaoh and how tenaciously the Pharaoh would fight against letting the Hebrew people leave Egypt. And would the Hebrews respond? When God told Moses that he should go to the people and say that the God of their fathers sent him to be their leader, Moses responded with consternation, "They will ask the name of this God who has commanded this humanly impossible exodus. What shall I say to them?"

I AM WHO I AM

Then God gave Moses His own name. It was not one of the various names that people had ascribed to Him to describe some aspect of what they observed of Him, like El Shaddai, the mighty God of the mountains. Instead, God gave Moses the name by which *He* wanted to be known, the name of His self-disclosure. "*I AM WHO I AM,*" He thundered. "Thus you shall say to the children of Israel, '*I AM* has sent me to you'" (Exod. 3:14).

The all-powerful name above all names for God is *HAYAH,* the causative Hebrew verb *to be* in the future tense, is rendered *YHWH,* or Yahweh—the Lord. In essence it means "to cause to happen." Our God is the verb and verve of all creation, humankind, and what He wills to occur. This name of God expresses His dynamic volition and thus is the name inherent in all His "I will" promises expressing His irrevocable intentionality. "I will be who I will be!" is God's word in His own self-designated name. "I will make to happen what I cause to happen."

The Need to Be Sure

Still, Moses was not sure. He knew the people would question the authenticity of his encounter with the One he now knew by His own name, Yahweh. He knew the disturbing question on his people's minds: "If God cares, why has all this suffering in Egypt come upon us? Is this Yahweh really in control of events and evil?"

To convince Moses, God gave him two very dramatic signs. God asked the fearful future liberator to throw his rod on the ground. It became a serpent, the very symbol of evil. God then commanded Moses to take the snake by the tail. When it became a rod again Moses knew that Yahweh was more powerful than evil and the evil incarnated in the Pharaoh and his vicious slave masters and mighty army.

Then Yahweh commanded Moses to put his hand on his chest inside his tunic. When Moses withdrew his hand, it was white as snow with leprosy. When Yahweh healed his leprous hand, Moses was ready to go back to Egypt to be His agent in setting His people free.

The account of the Exodus is filled with "I will" promises given by Yahweh and fulfilled by Him. All that Yahweh did—in wrenching His people out of the Pharaoh's grip, the parting of the sea, the constant provision during the journey to Mount Sinai—was so He could forge His people into a great nation whose life would be ruled by Him and guided by His commandments. At Sinai, He gave the Ten Commandments, five for their relationship with Him and five for their relationship with one another. The Decalogue begins with His all-powerful name, *I AM, YAHWEH.* "Yahweh, your God, who brought you out of the land of Egypt, out of the house of bondage" is the One who gives the commandments. Yahweh, who makes things happen, set irrevocable commandments for the obedience of those who are to receive His promised blessings.

What Does All This Mean for Us?

What does all this mean to us as we endure the storms of life, waiting for a rainbow? Plenty. In fact, everything. Yahweh is the headwater source from whom all of the "I will" promises in Scripture flow and finally surge down in the rainbow-orbed cataracts of Christ's "I will" promises.

Yahweh is in charge. This is the bracing impact of His name and how He operates. We can't change the unchangeable nature of God. He makes things happen in His way and in His timing. Nor can He be pushed around or manipulated by us to do things our way. Eventually our tune must change from "I'll do it my way," to "I'll do it His way!" Yahweh will be what He will be! His commandments have not gone out of style.

This itself is a rainbow in the storms of the moral relativism of our times. It's a whiff of clean fresh air wafting a scent of purity into the polluted values and distortions we breathe most of the time. We need this when we are tempted to forget that *holiness* is not a negative, prudish word but the robust, intentional lifestyle of a person who is liberated by a holy God.

Yahweh's rainbow also dispels the storm of judging Him and telling Him what is the best and most that can happen. We are reminded that the best that can happen is for us to be in deep fellowship with Him forever. The worst that can happen is that we should miss the reason we were born and come to the end of our physical lives destined to spend eternity separated from Him.

This puts into perspective the good things we sometimes deify and the bad things we abhor. The associations, accomplishments, and accouterments of our life are not better than knowing and loving God. Likewise, the suffering and disappointments of life are nothing in comparison to the worst that can happen— to miss the joy of life now and forever.

There is no freedom from panic and agitated worry until we really believe that Yahweh can and will use everything, working it into His plan and purpose for us. And while we wait, we rest in the positive things we've discovered about Yahweh, even in the storm. Then we can say expectantly, "God is cookin' up a rainbow!"

A Reason to Be Expectant

True expectancy is rooted in something much deeper than wishing or yearning. It is hope based on the greatest gift God desires to give us.

There's nothing more important than this gift. With it life is sublime; without it there is constant stress. It is the secret of true success, the source of wisdom beyond our understanding, the strength to endure in hard times. It's our ultimate goal, life's greatest privilege, and our most urgent need.

This is a gift many of us have difficulty receiving. It's not just facts or theories or ideas or carefully worded theology. It cannot be earned, and yet it is the one thing that should demand our constant attention and be the focus of our lives. It is of more value than human power, positions, or portfolios. And yet, nothing is more needed in the storms of life.

The history of God's covenant people could be charted in God's repeated effort to give this awesome gift. From Mount Sinai to the claiming of the Promised Land; from the establishment of the kingdom to the division into the separate kingdoms of Judah and Israel; from the decline of both kingdoms through syncretistic apostasy to the judgment of the exile; from the return from exile to the rebuilding of Jerusalem; from the turbulent days of vassalage under one conqueror after another—God sought to give this quality. The sins of the people came from a lack of it. Truth and mercy were forgotten because it was neglected. The

61

lowest points of defeat and suffering in the history of the covenant people over the centuries were because they rejected it.

Knowledge of God

What is this gift? Knowledge of God. The purpose and passion for which we were created are to know God. There is no vibrant expectancy without the knowledge of God. This knowledge of God determines the extent of expectation of His repeated rainbows of covenant faithfulness.

Many Christians admit that they do not really *know* God. For other believers, lack of knowledge of God is the cause of vacillating spirituality, inconsistency between the talk and walk of faith, and ineffectiveness in prayer. For still others, inadequate knowledge of God accounts for the reluctant response to holy living and moral responsibility. Like God's people in the Old Testament, often truth and mercy, faithfulness and kindness, as well as social righteousness are missing because we do not know God.

What does it mean to know God and live with a knowledge of Him? It involves both intimacy and integrity. The intimacy of the Thou-I relationship we were created to experience with God requires the opening of our innermost being to Him just as He has revealed His innermost nature to us. The word *intimacy* means "proceeding from within, inward, internal." In Hebrew the word for knowledge has the same root as "to know." It is also used for the physical and spiritual oneness of a husband and wife.

Knowledge of God is more than ideas about Him. It involves our total inner selves: intellect, emotion, and will. God knows all about what's going on inside us—we cannot hide from Him. The beginning of our knowledge of God, our relationship with Him, is when we know that we are known. So the psalmist says, "O LORD, You have searched me and known me" (Ps. 139:1). The psalmist yields his inner being to God when he realizes he is known by

God, "Search me, O God, and know my heart; / Try me and know my anxieties; / And see if there is any wicked way in me, / And lead me in the way of everlasting" (Ps. 139:23–24). Both understanding and awareness of God are met in response to our being known absolutely and thoroughly by Him.

Knowing God also is dependent on our integrity. The word means wholeness, undivided, unimpaired—completeness. Integrity is congruity of behavior, consistency between what we believe and what we do. Intimacy with God, knowing Him as He has revealed Himself, must be inseparably intertwined with His character and commandments. He has chosen to be our God and elected us to be His people. Knowing Him therefore requires our integrity and congruity of a life of faithfulness. Obedience is a vital secret of a growing knowledge of God.

The Real Cause of Panic

The real cause of the panic we've referred to previously is our lack of knowledge of God that involves both intimacy and integrity. When we have not yielded our inner selves to be known by God, and when we have not made knowing His loving kindness, faithfulness, and righteousness the purpose and passion of our lives, we react to the changes and crises of life with panic. Also, when we know that our lives are out of sync with the Lord because we lack integrity and congruity between our beliefs and behavior, we tend to feel estranged from God when we need Him.

A sign in the elevator I rode in a skyscraper said, "In case of an emergency, don't be alarmed; just press the panic button." Someone used to reacting with panic to the emergencies of life must have written this sign.

It's difficult not to panic in the face of trouble or adversity. Some people react to almost everything with panic. It affects the rest of us when unexpected tragedies hit or we are faced with threatening illness in ourselves or those we love. Also, panic surges in us when we confront situations that make demands on us we think are beyond our strength or understanding.

Whenever I do a survey of the needs of the people in my radio and television audiences, I am amazed at how often the word *panic* is used. One person wrote, "If I could claim a promise it would be for peace instead of panic. In the midst of life's worst trials, I'm anxious and in a panic." Another wrote, "I need healing of fear and panic when facing uncertainties." Still another wrote, "When crises hit, my first reaction is panic. It's like icy fingers around my soul. I actually shiver inside."

The great need we all share is to get prepared before panic strikes. Knowledge of God, intimacy, and integrity with Him, is the only way. This builds up a healthy memory of how He has helped us in the past and assures us that not even our failures and mistakes will make Him turn down our pleas for help.

Some of the "I will" promises Yahweh made to the people of Judah prior to and during the exile are strong antidotes to panic. The prophets who ministered to the covenant people spoke Yahweh's rainbow promises in the midst of the panic of the demise of Jerusalem, the fall of the southern kingdom, and the subsequent exile. These prophets had the burden of communicating Yahweh's judgment on their lack of intimacy with Him, which caused their apostasy and the absence of integrity. And yet Yahweh affirmed His covenant willingness to help His people. He promises no less to you and me.

Fear Not!

One of the most powerful "I will" rainbow promises to prepare us for the storms of life when we might be tempted to panic is Isaiah 41:9b, 10, 13:

I have chosen you and have not cast you away;
Fear not, for I am with you;
Be not dismayed, for I am your God.
I will strengthen you,
Yes, I will help you,
I will uphold you with My righteous right hand. . . .
For I, the LORD your God, will hold your right hand,
Saying to you, "Fear not, I will help you."

Note the antidotes for the poison of panic. The word *dismayed* translates a Hebrew word that actually means, "look about, cast about." The words *I Am* translate "Yahweh." So, "Yahweh is with you. Don't look around furtively, don't cast about with trepidation, seeking help from anything or anyone else!"

And what Yahweh offered the people of Judah in a perilous time He offers us: His own strength and help. And don't miss the dynamic intimacy in which these precious gifts are given. The Lord offers to take our right hand with His right hand. He could stand beside us taking our left hand in His right hand. Instead, He takes our right hand and holds us with eye-to-eye intensity. This is what He does for us when our first reaction to problems is to pray rather than panic.

A New Beginning

In communion with the Lord, He gives us a further "I will" promise that splashes the rainbow on our fearful hearts.

Do not remember the former things,
Nor consider the things of old.
Behold, *I will do* a new thing,
Now it shall spring forth;
Shall you not know it?

Isaiah 43:18–19, italics added

The Lord will bring us through the storm and His covenant rainbow, "I will do a new thing," gives us the courage we need. He will give us a new chance, a fresh beginning, an opportunity to begin again. The creativity of God is inexhaustible. He gives us the power to let go of the former things, including our sins and mistakes, but also our achievements that fail to sustain us in the stormy times.

To be able to forget the former things is not easy. It requires repentance. This was difficult for the people of Judah. They tried to hold on to their former glory and grandeur and found it hard to confess their sin, apostasy, and idolatry. God had not left them, but they had displaced Him for the idols of their hearts. By their actions they told God that He was wrong and they were right. His promise of a new beginning fell on ears deafened by pride.

Their breach with God widened. When Jerusalem and the southern kingdom were invaded and sacked, the people felt forsaken. Other nations ridiculed them and called them by the name "Forsaken." God had not forsaken His people; they had forsaken Him. But God did not give up on His people. His mercy outstretched His judgment. When His people would not come to Him, He reached across the breach they had created.

During the dark, stormy days of the devastation of Jerusalem and the ravage of the land by foes, God gave another promise of a new beginning. "You shall no longer be termed Forsaken, / Nor your land any more be termed Desolate; / But you shall be called Hephzibah, and your land Beulah; / For the LORD delights in you" (Isa. 62:4). After the judgment of the exile, God promised to restore Jerusalem and heal the breach between Him and His people.

He offered Israel a new name. Hephzibah means "My delight is in her." Imagine! Instead of "Forsaken," God's people will be called by a name that expresses His delight in them. And their land that had been termed Desolate would now be called Beulah, meaning "married to the Lord again." God would not desert His people, His bride. Again we feel the indomitable persistence of God to reach across the breach and reconcile His people.

In our stormy days, lashed about by the tornadoes of feeling forsaken, we too need a new name. Especially when we imagine a breach between us and God because of our sins and failures, our anguish must be overcome by a sense of God's indefatigable delight in us in spite of what we've done or been. Across the breach He calls us by a new given name, Hephzibah. And in response, we can express our delight in being forgiven and offered a new beginning.

So What's New?

I have a friend who has a jovial, almost jocular way of greeting people. Without saying, "Hello," or "How are you?" he just blurts out, "So what's new?" It's such a habit that he doesn't expect an answer. I enjoy catching him off-guard with, "Really want to know?" and then I launch into a long answer that's a lot more than he expected or bargained for.

My friend's question, however, is one we should be able to answer with new experiences of God's goodness and grace that are being distilled into our knowledge of Him.

A New Heart

This ever-increasing knowledge of God flows into a heart that's constantly being renewed. It was Ezekiel, first called into his prophetic ministry to the exiles in Babylonia with a vision of the glory of God "like the appearance of a rainbow in a cloud on a rainy day" (Ezek. 1:28), who was used by God to prophesy the gift of a new heart for His people. After long years of ministry in Babylon, when all hope seemed lost, Ezekiel was given a promise for God's covenant people. It's a promise for us when we're tempted to give up.

67

Listen to the Voice of the rainbow-radiant glory and assurance of God. "I will give you a new heart and put a new spirit within you; I will take the heart of stone out of your flesh and give you a heart of flesh. I will put My Spirit within you and cause you to walk in My statutes, and you will keep My judgments and do them" (Ezek. 36:26–27).

This is exactly what we need in cloudy, stormy times of discouragement. When our strength is spent and we've exhausted our resources, God promises to break up the hard stone of hopelessness and give us a new heart that is capable of receiving His own Spirit. He knows that He must have a new person for a new beginning. *He* is not interested in making old things a little bit better, but in making *us* new.

A New Covenant

To create new people to be filled with His Spirit required a new covenant, a transforming, cosmic atonement for humankind. God never gives up. When His covenant people rebelled and persisted in sin, the Lord was planning the greatest rainbow of all—the sending of His Son, the cross, resurrection, and Pentecost.

Through Jeremiah the Lord said,

> Behold, the days are coming . . . when I will make a new covenant with the house of Israel and with the house of Judah. . . . This is the covenant I will make . . . I will put My law in their minds, and write it on their hearts; and I will be their God, and they shall be My people. No more shall every man teach his neighbor, and every man his brother, saying, "Know the LORD," for they all shall know Me, from the least of them to the greatest of them. . . . for I will forgive their iniquity, and their sin I will remember no more.
>
> Jeremiah 31:31, 33–34

Two wondrous truths flash from that spectacular rainbow promise: first, the Lord's indefatigable desire to make Himself known to us, and second, His desire that we fulfill our awesome destiny to really know Him. And this promise was made at the darkest time of Israel's history. I like to couple it with another "I will" promise that impels us to respond. "Call to Me, and I will answer you, and show you great and mighty things, which you do not know" (Jer. 33:3).

When we do call in the storm, God's answer is the rainbow of His Son. In Him, the knowledge of God begins and never ends. Jesus Christ is the rainbow over the breach from the heart of God to our hearts.

Coming to
the Point

"Lord, if You are willing. . . ." Then Jesus put out His hand and touched him, saying, "I am willing."

Matthew 8:2–3

A nd now we come to our basic thrust. The God who said, "I set my rainbow in the cloud," four thousand years later said, "This is My beloved Son, in whom I am well pleased" (Matt. 3:17). Christ Himself is God's rainbow set in the clouds of human sin and suffering. He is the Father's reach across the breach, spanning from His heart to our hearts. All of God's "I will" promises we've considered are intimations of the Incarnation when the preexistent Word revealed His willingness to help and heal us.

So here's the secret: Christ is our rainbow. With burning-bush, I-Am, Yahweh authority, He said, "I am the way, the truth, and the life. No one comes to the Father except through Me" (John 14:6). He doesn't just show the way, He is the way. He doesn't only tell us truth about the Father, He is the truth of the Father. He doesn't simply exemplify how life was meant to be lived, He is the very life of God with us.

The more we know of Christ the more we know of God. "For it pleased the Father that in Him all the fullness should dwell, and by Him to reconcile all things to Himself, by Him, whether things on earth or things in heaven, having made peace through the blood of His cross" (Col. 1:19–20).

If Christ is our rainbow reconciling us to the Father, our in-Person new covenant, our Lord in whom we abide, and who abides in us—what does that do to Matheson's image of climbing the

73

rainbow? It magnificently personalizes it. Christ comes to us and takes us by the hand and heart and leads us to the Father.

Listen to Matheson's own words, "Whether You come in sunshine or rain, I take You to my heart joyfully. You are Yourself more than the sunshine; You are Yourself compensation for rain. It is You and not Your gifts I crave." Christ Himself was Matheson's rainbow and climbing the rainbow for him meant claiming what Christ promised.

There are fifteen cloud-dispersing "I will" promises made to us by Christ. They express His gracious willingness to reach us where we are and give us inexplicable joy. These are tender words that touch us when we hurt and inspire us when we long to hope again. We will claim each of these in this and the following chapters.

Coming to the Point

Christ comes to us at the point of our need and helps us to come to the point. He encourages us to be specific about our deepest needs. Dynamic prayer is getting to the point about the point of our need. Christ knows that His abundant willingness, coupled with our willing response, will enable us to experience Him as our rainbow in the rain.

This is vividly illustrated in Matthew's account of Jesus' encounter with a leper immediately following the delivery of the Sermon on the Mount. A couple of years ago, I went to the Mount of Beatitude overlooking the Sea of Galilee and tried to recapture how it happened. As I sat there meditating on Matthew's account, the scene was replayed in my imagination.

Jesus spoke with immense authority and incredible compassion. As I listened, in my mind's eye I watched the faces of the people seated on the grassy hillside. The disciples were riveted by what the Master was saying. The multitudes of people listened with rapt attention and amazement. The faces of the scribes and Pharisees exposed their discomfort with the Galilean carpenter's radical teaching.

Then, off away from the crowds, I pictured a man who was forbidden to mingle with the crowd. He was rejected by the others and kept at a safe distance. I could see, even at a distance, the telltale white spots of his loathed disease. The man was a leper. Untouchable!

Then I caught his face. It was radiant with appreciation and devotion for the Master. I sensed that the words of Jesus were like arms of love gathering him up with acceptance, drawing the man to His heart. Though the pitiful victim knew he could never touch or be touched by another person as long as he lived, Jesus seemed to reach out and touch him with His words. The leper felt cared for even at a distance.

A wish began to grow inside the leper. It grew to a compelling desire. Somehow, he had to make personal contact with Jesus. He had heard of His healing miracles. People with all kinds of diseases were healed by the touch of His powerful hand. Would He touch an untouchable leper? The man had to find a way to meet Him and find out if His compassion and healing power would be extended to him.

The leper knew there were two roads leading down from the mount. If Jesus took one of them, he could take the other road, circle around, and be waiting for Him to come by on the way to Capernaum. When the Master finished speaking and the rest of the people were talking excitedly about what they heard, the leper watched carefully to see which road Jesus would take. Sure enough, Jesus headed in the direction he expected. The leper hobbled away as fast as his sore, blistered feet would take him. He made it to the bottom of the hillside and was there waiting on the Capernaum road as Jesus, with the throng crowding behind Him, approached.

75

Picture it as I did. Capture the scene. According to the Law of Moses, the leper was required to cry out, "Unclean! Unclean!" whenever he was in a crowd. When he cried out, the crowd stopped in its tracks. There he was in the middle of the road. How could they get around him without any physical contact? Only Jesus continued to walk toward the leper. It was as if He expected the man to be there. Jesus' movement toward him unleashed the leper's pent-up emotions. He ran to Jesus, fell at His feet, and worshiped Him. The crowd had not expressed such adoration. But this man knew two things: He had a terrible need and he believed that Jesus could heal him.

The leper quickly came to the point about the point of his need. "Lord, if You are willing, You can make me clean."

The crowd murmured with disdain mingled with intense interest in how Jesus would respond. They knew well that it was against the law to touch the man. Yet when Jesus had healed others, He laid His hands on them. What would the Master do?

There seemed to be no question in Jesus' mind about what to do. He touched the leper! Oh, how wonderful to be touched! As Jesus held him, He spoke with profound love and compassion: "I am willing; be cleansed."

The leper's eyes were held by Jesus' eyes filled with grace. But what authority flashed from those eyes! Then slowly, as if hoping against hope, the man looked down on his hands. The leprosy was gone! He was healed. Excitement rippled through the crowd, but it was nothing in comparison to the joy the leper felt. Then He did something he had not been able to do for years—touch another person. He touched Jesus! He was healed not only of the leprosy, but of his estrangement, rejection, and lack of contact with others. The crowd murmured, "This is no ordinary rabbi or teacher or even healer. Only God's Spirit could do the healing through Him."

The leper had come to the point about the point of his deepest need. His willingness to dare to be specific had been met by the willingness of the divine Son of God.

The Willingness of Christ

As I finished my reflection on what happened to the leper after the Sermon on the Mount, I sat for a long time, thinking about the unqualified willingness of Christ to meet me at the point of my need, if I would come to the point with Him about it.

Does my hearing of the radical truth of the Sermon on the Mount bring me rushing to Jesus' feet to worship and come to the point of my need? I realized the words of the Lord had become very familiar to me through years of study and preaching. But that day I heard them with new ears.

Were the qualities of the Beatitudes part of my character? Was my light of faith shining before people or under a bushel? Did I love my enemies? And what about my prayer life? Was it really as deep as Jesus mandated? How often public prayer and leadership of worship was more important than prolonged time alone with the Lord. How serious was I about letting Him control my life? My own need for control of people, my church, my future, was threatened by Jesus' call for complete commitment.

Next, Jesus' words about worry and anxiety hit me. How often I'd preached to others about Christ's power to help us manage stress. What would my family, close friends, people who work with and for me—what would they say about my own stress level? Was I really seeking first the kingdom? I wrote books about that, but was I living it?

The concluding words of the Master, "Not everyone who says to Me, 'Lord, Lord' shall enter the kingdom of heaven," challenged my facile talk about my faith. And the Lord's parable about the man who built his house on sand and the other on rock pressed me to a searching question: Was my life and ministry based on the solid rock of Christ or on the sand of my own talents, techniques, and management skills?

Confrontation

In the quiet of this confrontation with my Lord's radical call to discipleship, I realized that I had drifted into a kind of bland unwillingness. It was like a low-grade fever. Not bad enough to make me realize that I was in danger, but serious enough to keep me from truly being a self-abandoned, ready-for-anything follower of Christ and leader of others.

Was I willing, like the leper? Reese Howell's words came to mind. When he was forced to face his need for a deeper relationship with Christ, he blurted out, "Lord, I'm just not willing!" To which Christ answered in his soul, "Reese, are you willing to be made willing?"

This was Christ's question to me that day on the Mount of Beatitude. I had come there to prepare a sermon I would preach to others. Instead, I heard the Son of God, my Master, Lord, and Savior, preach to me. And then, in reading on about the leper in the opening of Matthew 8, I saw something I'd never considered before: the close connection of the Sermon on the Mount in chapters 5–7 with the amazing healing, when Jesus touched one who was untouchable.

Did it happen the way I imagined it? Little matter. What did matter was that the Holy Spirit enabled me to see the link between hearing Christ's words and being willing to really worship Him and come to the point of my own need for healing. Could I throw myself down before the Lord? "I need to be changed, Lord, if You are willing. . . ."

This is exactly what I did. I walked to the edge of the Mount, looking out over the sea. I got down on my knees. "Lord, I'm willing . . . really willing . . . if You are willing." And He was. He always is when we come to the point about the real point of our need for Him.

Divine Volition

I have recounted this crucial event in my life some years ago because it personally illustrates the dynamic power of volition: Christ's willingness motivating my willingness. When Christ said to the leper, "I am willing," it expressed, "I will" in the strongest possible sense.

We are endowed with the faculty of will. It links us with Christ, the Word, the revelation of the volitional power of the Godhead. In the beginning, the Word chose to create. Later, He chose not to totally obliterate humanity with the flood, but chose to enter into the process of saving His fallen rebellious children. He chose to set a rainbow in the cloud. And He chose to come as the incarnate Word, the Messiah, Savior, and Lord.

Christ is the will of God for us: The revelation in His humanity as Son of Man of the willingness God wants for all humankind, and what willingness He has to heal, redeem, and save us. Each time Yahweh spoke the forceful "I will" promises through Israel's history, it was the Word who spoke from the heart of the Father. And in Christ we behold the Word Himself, the Father's will appealing to our will.

C. G. Jung said that we don't really understand Christ until we grapple with His focused emphasis on the will. I agree. And I would add that it is through the liberating power of the cross that our wills are set free to accept the love the Father offers us.

Grace begets willingness and willingness appropriates the unlimited blessing Christ has been authorized by the Father to give us through the Holy Spirit. Christ is the dynamic center—the willingness of the Father to redeem and reconcile us, the One who baptizes us with the Spirit. All if we are willing to receive.

Rainbows of Hope

Rainbows of hope and a new beginning are the direct result of Christ's response to our willingness to accept His greater willingness to love, encourage, and bless us. And as we have stressed: Christ our rainbow appears not just after the rain but while it is still storming. Unlike nature's evanescent rainbows, He does not fade or vanish. "I will be with you always . . . never leave . . . never forsake."

But I must be honest and also share that it's when we come to the point with Christ about the point of our need in the storm of any day, any hour, that we can see the rainbow. Are we so used to seeing nature's rainbows at the end of a storm that we find it difficult to think of Christ's presence as our rainbow assurance in the rain?

Add to this our quick-solution complex of today. We want results. Resolution. Change according to our desires when we want it. The secret of serenity is to wait for things to work out because we already have a renewed relationship with Christ, who alone can work things out. We stumble over our mistaken translation of Romans 8:28, "And we know that all things work together for good to those who love God, to those who are the called according to His purpose." The correct rendering of the Greek should be, "For we know that God works all things together for good to those who love Him, to the called according to His purpose." Quite a difference. And it is Christ who is the agent of working things for our good and His glory. If . . .

The Big IF

Well, there we are again. *If.* Yes, if we are willing to get to the point with Him about the point of our need right now. The leper asked Jesus if He was willing. Christ wants to know about our willingness to trust Him.

What is it for you? Down beneath all of the surface needs, what is the aching need? Way down inside?

Get to the point about the point of your need right now.

We have an immense proclivity to hang on to our needs, to try to handle them ourselves. Or we just push them down inside and endure them without actually releasing them to the Lord. We can go to church, read our Bibles, try to live the best we can, but in our prayers we seldom talk to the Lord about the real issues on our minds and hearts or allow Him to raise them. We get used to storms and clouds and do not expect the rainbow.

Are You Receiving What You Need?

I talked to a man at a conference in Canada where I was speaking. Over lunch, I asked, "Well, are you receiving what the Lord brought you here to receive from Him?"

The man looked surprised. "Never thought of it that way," he responded. "I've been to lots of renewal conferences like this. They're inspiring all right, but I've never expected the Lord to do for me the kind of spiritual miracles with problems some of these people here talk about. Some things you just have to live with," he continued glumly.

Seated next to the man was his very grim, religiously proper wife with a stern look on her face. I sensed that the man's marriage was what he had decided he "had to live with." So I engaged the two of them in a conversation about them, their life together, their hopes and vision for the future. Then it all came out. Tension, lack of affection, some tough times in which they blamed each other.

We lingered over lunch into the middle of the afternoon. I shared some of the discoveries Mary Jane and I made in difficult times. I also confided what we were learning about keeping romance alive in a lifetime marriage.

The dining room was empty now except for the four of us: the man and his wife, me . . . and the Lord. The couple talked about the hurts of the years. After lots of tears, I realized they were at the point of their real need and were ready to pray. Their willingness to receive made it possible for the Lord to heal their marriage.

At the end of the conference, I walked the couple to their car. They were headed home, a new couple. As I held the door open for the woman, she whispered in my ear, "Thanks. We've had a second honeymoon. Maybe the first one, really!"

Watching them drive away, I prayed "Thank You, Lord, for bringing them to the point with You about the real point of their need." And then I wondered how many people were leaving the conference essentially the same as they had come. I think of this often when I greet people after worship on Sunday morning. The question I'd like to ask each person is, "Well, did you get to the point with the Lord?"

Getting to the Point about Struggles

I didn't have to ask a single young mother with whom I had several long conversations about her struggles raising three young children alone. Her prayers had been for a husband to be a partner and a father to her children. She was so obsessed with these concerns that she had allowed her relationship with the Lord to drift.

One Sunday, at the conclusion of the worship, she responded to the invitation to come forward to pray with one of the pastors or elders. Because of our previous conversation, she came to me.

"I realized this morning," she confided quietly, "that I have been asking the Lord for everything except what I need most of all. I really need to love and know Him for Himself as my Lord, not for what He will do for me. I want to give my life to Him. A relationship with Him is my real need. With that I think I can really trust Him for the secondary things." The woman had gotten to the point.

Not a Once-Done Thing

Coming to the point with Christ is not a "once-done thing." We need to be totally honest with Him every day. I shared my experience of coming to the point many years ago on the Mount of Beatitudes. But this was not the first of such times of being brought to a willingness to claim His willingness to help me. And the same thing has often happened since.

I have become so keenly aware of coming to the point of my real need and allowing the Lord to get to the point about what He knows are deeper needs He wants to expose and heal, that I end my daily time alone with Him with the specific question, "Lord, have I gotten to the point? Have I let You make Your point with Me?"

Sometimes I realize I've avoided or missed the real point and have to remain in prayer until I can say, "If You are willing . . ." Then I hear Him sound in my soul, "I am willing." Then what follows is suited for the surrendered need—"You are forgiven," or "I have heard your cry for help; I will carry the burden," or "Yes, I will give you the strength you need." The response is always specific and directly applicable to the problem or possibility.

It's in these times that I see, know, and can claim the rainbow in the rain. Nothing may be changed yet, but everything's different.

As I close this chapter, I hope you are saying, "Okay, Lloyd, I got to the point."

But more than that, in this moment before you read on, I pray you will come to the point about your deepest need with Christ. "Lord, I know You are willing to help me. I'm willing."

I promise you that with His renewed touch you will experience His special rainbow.

5

Outstretched Arms

The one who comes to Me I will by no means cast out.

John 6:37

I went to the airport to meet a friend's plane. As I stood in the crowd at the gate waiting for him, I saw a couple I knew standing close to the door. They were in an intense conversation, so I didn't approach them.

As I observed them, it seemed as if they were rehearsing something, repeatedly stretching out their arms toward the door. I surmised what that meant. They were getting ready to welcome home their daughter. They wanted to be sure that the moment she saw them she would see their faces and the gesture of their outstretched arms as a sign of their reassuring acceptance.

Their daughter had left home two years before as a result of a rift with her parents. They had not heard from her during this time and all efforts to locate her had failed. Then one day a letter arrived from the young woman. She explained the sad tale of a brief romance, the birth of a child, the difficulties she was facing as a young single parent in a strange city, and the alarming details of her failures and brokenness. She asked if she could come home.

Her parents immediately sent a telegram telling her how lonesome they were for her, how much they loved her, and that they wanted her to come home with her child. They wired her airfare and arranged for a flight to Los Angeles.

Now the time had come and the parents were anxious to communicate unqualified love and unrestrained joy at their daughter's homecoming.

When the passengers streamed out of the passageway from the plane, the parents kept their arms outstretched. Finally, as one of the last passengers off the plane, there was their daughter and granddaughter.

Her face was clouded with caution and uncertainty. Then she burst into tears of relief when she saw her parents with their radiant faces of love and outstretched arms of acceptance running to her and their grandchild.

Some months later, after a healing reconciliation with her parents and a new beginning of faith in Christ, the young mother shared with me how she felt that day at the airport.

"I'll never forget those outstretched arms reaching out to me when I least deserved them," she said.

"That's the way Christ greets us whenever we return to Him. His arms are always outstretched to receive us," I responded.

"I hope I never forget that," she said wistfully.

"You probably will," I confided. "We all do, often. But the time between when you forget and remember again will get shorter. There doesn't need to be a long time of remorse and self-condemnation when we fail. Christ is with us all the time. He never stiff-arms our return to Him or folds His arms in disdain."

An "I Will" Rainbow Promise

Christ has given us an "I will" rainbow promise for times when the dark clouds of regret and self-incrimination cover the sky of our self-perception. He parts the clouds just enough for the quickening ray of His love to shine through to refract the rain with this rainbow assurance, "The one who comes to Me I will by no means cast out" (John 6:37).

In this promise, Jesus' use of a strong double negative actually equals a great positive. The phrase "by no means" might be translated "No! No! Absolutely not." The margin reference of the New King James Version adds "certainly not." In the most forceful way possible, Jesus tells us He will not reject anyone who comes to Him regardless of what that person has been, said, or done. He will never turn His back on us; He will never cast us out. Christ's inviting, yearning, appealing, saving arms are always outstretched to you and me. Whoever will may come. Whenever. However. No exceptions.

Chosen to Come

This "I will" rainbow promise is given because we have been chosen to come to Christ. Note the propitious prelude to this promise: "All that the Father gives Me will come to Me." The rainbow flashes with greater brilliance as these words grip us.

You and I are the Father's gift to Christ, the Son! We are chosen, elected, predestined by the Father to be Christ's disciples. Of course, we have to choose to accept our chosenness, but we are able to make this choice because of God's prior election of us. And the Father gives us to the Son so He may love us as He loves the Son. Awesome!

This is the rainbow assurance of the Father's covenant, His promise to be our God. He has given us to Christ so Christ may pursue, woo, capture our hearts to make us one with Him and the Father.

Christ's rainbow promise to "never, never" cast us out or let us go commands our attention as He explains His responsibility for you and me. He will never give up on us. We are His assignment from the Father. It is His task to see us through the ups and downs of life and get us safely into heaven. Look at this persistent rainbow:

> For I came down from heaven, not to do My own will, but the will of Him who sent Me. This is the will of the Father who sent *Me*, that of all He has given to Me I should lose nothing, but should raise it up at the last day. And this the will of Him who sent *Me*, that everyone who sees the Son and believes in Him may have everlasting life; and I will raise him up at the last day.
>
> John 6:38–40, italics added

This lasting splendor of rainbow grace assures us that Christ is determined not to lose us. We can't drift beyond His reach across the breach of our failures and mistakes. With dogged persistence He tracks us, with divine omniscience He finds us, and with indefatigable grace He forgives our sins and heals our broken hearts.

For good reason. The best of all reasons: that we may be sure we have everlasting life. The term means more than "in perpetuity." It is life to the fullest now with a perpetual flow of the Spirit of Christ in us. Then on our "last day," either the decisive day of Christ's return or the day of our physical demise, He may resurrect our reformed spirits to reign with Him in heaven.

Our startling discovery is that Christ actually uses our failures and mistakes as occasions for our growth in His grace. Repeatedly, it's the sight of the rainbow, "I will never cast you out," which gives us a chance for new beginnings. It's in the context of His unchanging covenant love that He helps us confront what we've done or been. Persistently He works with us to help us discover the deeper causes and patiently encourages us to confess them to Him along with the specific failure or mistake. His arms of forgiveness are always outstretched so we can come to Him and be embraced as those reassuring arms enfold us. Overcome by His grace, we resolve to trust Him more deeply in our decisions, actions, and reactions.

The Story of John

Allow me to illustrate this by relating the true account of how a Scottish friend of mine, John Muldrin, first experienced the wonder of this "I will" rainbow promise—"I will by no means cast you out"—and how it has provided reassurance in his growth in Christ.

I first met John two years ago at Loch Hope in the farthest north reaches of the Highlands of Scotland, where Mary Jane and I went to fish for sea trout following my summer study leave. He served as our *gillie* (guide) for a week of fly-fishing. Patiently he taught Mary Jane how to use a fly rod and corrected some errors in my casting ability. With his help we caught some fish and had a wonderful time on the magnificently beautiful loch.

John appeared to be a jovial man, always ready with a steady flow of jokes, folklore, and fishing stories. Since we fished from a boat, there was plenty of time to talk about a wide range of subjects, including Christianity. We purposely refrained from telling John I am a clergyman because we wanted whatever we might be able to say about our love for Christ to be taken as authentic, rather than the expected, religious thing for church leaders to say. We wanted to witness to our faith in a natural, relaxed way.

When John let his guard down I sensed an immense sadness underneath his jovial exterior. As the week progressed I suspected that the Lord may have planned our time with him for a greater purpose than a week of rest and fishing.

One day, near the end of our week, Mary Jane decided not to fish, but to remain at the small hotel. So John and I headed off for Loch Hope.

After loading our rods into the boat, we pushed off and rowed a distance from the shore. Instead of handing me my rod with a recommendation of the right fly for the day, John looked at me intently and said, "Lloyd, I've been watching you and Mary Jane all week. There's something different about you. I've been trying to sort it out. You seem very happy, but it's more than that. When you talk about the Lord, it sounds as if you really know Him."

As the boat drifted up the loch, inside I prayed, "Lord, help me to introduce John to You!"

Then John started telling me his life story—a story of broken dreams, unfulfilled hopes, and unrealized plans for his life. John was discouraged, hovering on the edge of alcohol addiction. Most of all, he felt empty inside and plagued with low self-esteem. As John finished telling me about himself, tears streamed down his face.

I shared my own story of meeting Christ and how He helped me deal with my own failures and mistakes through the years. I empathized with John's feeling unworthy of the Lord's love as well as the false notion that he could earn a place with Him by being good enough. After a thorough review of the basics of the cross, forgiveness, and how to be born again, I quoted the verse we've been considering, "The one who comes to *Me* I will by no means cast out" and told him about Christ's outstretched arms.

This hooked our fisherman John. "You mean, in spite of everything I can come to Christ right now? I can literally experience this love, joy, and peace you've been talking about?"

"Yes, John," I replied warmly. "You are loved, forgiven, and can begin a new life now!"

I'll never forget what happened. John got on his knees in the boat and prayed one of the most moving prayers of faith and commitment I've ever heard. Afterward, his face was radiant with joy and excitement. He couldn't stop talking about the sheer delight he felt. There was little fishing done the rest of the day. We were too busy talking about Christ.

On the way back to the hotel, I told John how important it would be for him to share his faith with others. "Tell someone today," I encouraged.

"Why don't I start with Mary Jane?" John responded with enthusiasm.

When we reached the hotel, Mary Jane poked her head out of the window of our room. "Catch any fish?" she asked.

"No," John blurted out with gusto. "But your husband caught a man!"

Mary Jane rushed down into the courtyard to hear the full account of what had happened to John and to encourage him in his new life.

Before we said good-bye to John at the end of the week, I shared with him what I was discovering about climbing the rainbow in the rain. This book was taking shape in my mind at the time, and I knew that there would be some cloudy, stormy days ahead for John as he tried to live his new faith. I explained how the rainbow promise that Christ would never, never let go of him would break through in even deeper ways in any dark days ahead. We promised to pray for each other as we anticipated the rainbows of Christ's assurance in whatever clouded our lives.

What then happened to John is the best part of the story. It shows that Christ's rainbow promise is crucial for those both beginning and growing in the Christian life.

Stinking Thinking

John recently told me that the challenge for him was to allow Christ to transform what he calls his "stinking thinking." Freed from any addiction to alcohol, he no longer needs to fear physically stinking because of overindulgence. However, he often has to deal with the reek of his thought patterns. "Stinking thinking" for John is the misperception that he has the right or the authority to level blame and subsequent punishment, especially on himself. This old habit is being healed. And Christ is doing it! Whenever the clouds of failure or mistakes hang heavy, John remembers Christ's special rainbow promise to him, "The one who comes to Me I will by no means cast out."

John has continued reflecting on rainbows in the clouds of life. He now names as rainbows all the surprising interventions of Christ he has received. He recently called me to tell me about two jobs he's been offered. One was to return to the executive world at a very good salary with many benefits, while the other was at half the salary helping the unemployed find meaningful work. He chose the position working with the unemployed because he can care for people the way Christ cares for him.

"Anyway, it has more benefits—the kind that last. One more rainbow!" John exclaimed.

The great thing about John's story is what it reveals to us about the volitional viability of Christ. He wills to receive fallible people like you and me. His promise to never cast us out is an ever-present rainbow when the clouds of self-doubt regather to darken any day with insecurity.

The Punitive Self

The outstretched arms of Christ beckon the punitive self within us that too often belittles our outer performing self. This part of our inner nature resists obedience to the first commandment. It seeks to be a god with the assumed authority of rendering judgment about our true worth. It keeps us so preoccupied with our inadequacies that we are distracted from the real issue:

sin, our separation from God. Christ breaks through this defensive wall and shows us the real need of our lives and offers outstretched arms for us to come to Him for healing grace, forgiveness, reconciliation, and a new life.

For some of us it's difficult to respond to Christ's outstretched arms. Too often we have tried to meet all the demands of this punitive self by never making mistakes or failing. Perfectionism sets in and pride results. We think of ourselves as good people who can keep all the rules. When the raging storm of some big failure hits, the punitive self is of little help. It chants, "If you'd only tried harder, worked more strenuously, done better, then this would not have happened." Pride blindfolds the eyes of our hearts from seeing the rainbow of grace and accepting the promise of "the one who comes to Me I will by no means cast out."

The punitive self is often the ready recruit of Satan's conniving strategies. He is the putdown manipulator. If he can make us so discouraged with ourselves that we can't imagine Christ's outstretched arms are for us, he wins, and the storm continues without a rainbow. But Christ is more powerful than Satan and his schemes of discouragement.

Christ will not let us continue in dark, stormy days for long. When we have no place to turn He gives us new eyes to see His rainbow and sounds in our souls: "Give Me your failures and mistakes. I love you. The Father elected you to be My disciple. You are My responsibility. Trust Me and you will make it through this tough time and on to My plans for you. What's more, as a result of what you've experienced, you will become My agent to give healing and hope to others enduring a dark time."

A Man's First Christmas

I witnessed the power of this "I will" promise in the life of a man who greeted me after worship last December with a joyous announcement. "This is my first Christmas!" he said with excitement.

The man had not been in a church service for years. He came to tell what happened to him. He was about forty-five years old, impeccably dressed, the image of a proper professional executive. With precise detail he relayed the reason for his joy.

"On Sunday morning, November 22," he said, "I was lower than I've ever been in my life. My wife asked for a separation and I'd moved into a hotel. After getting over blaming her, I faced my own failure in the most important human relationship of my life. This brought me to the deepest discouragement I've ever experienced.

"I don't handle failure very well," the man continued. "I was raised in a religious family and taught all the rules. Success was top priority. If my parents ever made mistakes, they never told me about them or helped me know what to do with mine. These past few years I've been obsessed with my job and earning a lot of money. In the midst of it all, my wife decided that no marriage was better than the empty one she had.

"So there I was in a hotel room alone, feeling incredible pain and loneliness. I started spinning the television dial looking for something to take my mind off my troubles and chanced onto your program. You were in the middle of a message. Just as I reached for the dial, you described me and how I was feeling. 'How does this guy know about me?' I wondered as I sat glued to the television set.

"You were talking about how to deal with failure and gave the example of a man who returned to Christ when his life fell apart. Then you paused and said, 'There are people here in this sanctuary and watching on television who are in great peril. They are trying to handle some big failure on their own strength. It won't work. If you think you have a corner on mistakes or are the most miserable failure around, Christ wants to help you get up from being down on yourself.' Then you quoted a promise from Christ that sent chills up my spine. After you finished I got the Gideon Bible out of the desk and read it. Remember what it was? 'The one who comes to Me I will by no means cast out'!"

Alone in his hotel room the man got on his knees to pray his first prayer in years. He responded to Christ's outstretched arms and committed his life to Him. When he told his wife about what happened to him, she was willing to have him come home. He knows he has challenging days ahead as he reprioritizes his life, but he also knows what to do when he gets off track.

"Now you see why I say this is my first Christmas," the man beamed. As his wife joined our conversation, she affirmed what her husband told me.

"Really, it's *our* first Christmas. I had drifted from Christ too. We're both so thankful that He came and comes to call all kinds of failures, even people like us who look like they are succeeding but are failing in what really counts."

Take No One for Granted

My own experience of Christ's offer of constant new beginnings has helped me take no one for granted.

A woman in my congregation needed to reaffirm her status with Christ. She complained about how difficult it was to pray and read the Bible. Worship seemed flat and she found herself very critical of her family and friends.

"What's been happening in your life recently?" I asked one day when she came to see me. After catching me up on her job and busy life, she said, "I can't understand it. I have made so many poor decisions and bad choices lately. As an experienced executive I should know better."

"Ever get down on yourself about these mistakes?" I gently asked.

"Oh sure," she responded. "In fact when I take time to pray, I find myself saying, 'Listen, you have no right to ask for guidance when you've messed up things so badly. If only you had done better on the guidance the Lord had given you before.'"

It didn't take long to help my friend see the connection between her self-judgment and her inability to experience the Lord's presence in her prayers. The Lord had not withdrawn from her; she had closed herself off as one unworthy of receiving fresh power in prayer.

Time for Another Rainbow

Do you ever have dark days of discouragement over your own failures and mistakes? You may be facing one of those times right now, or are you not really over the last one that hit you? If so, it's time for another rainbow, a new experience of Christ's outstretched arms. Even if you've been a Christian for years, Christ will never close His outstretched arms in a gesture of disdain over your failures and mistakes. He'll never give up on you.

Not now. Not ever!

6

The Longing to Escape When the Going Gets Rough

I will give you rest.

Matthew 11:28

*D*o you ever long to escape when the going gets rough? Of course. All of us want to escape at one time or another. And for lots of different reasons. To get away from our problems and challenges. To leave a demanding but unfulfilling job. To retreat from a stressful relationship. To take "time out" from a difficult marriage. To walk out of a seemingly impossible situation. To move out of a troubled city. To stop feeling responsible for social justice.

We can empathize with the psalmist: "Oh, that I had wings like a dove! / I would fly away and be at rest. . . . / I would hasten my escape / From the windy storm and tempest" (Ps. 55:6, 8). But what kind of rest would this be?

When the Going Is Rough

A friend wrote me, "I'm anxious and fearful about living in Los Angeles. My basic instinct and wish is to sell everything and move out of this city. The gangs and racial tensions scare me to death."

Will escape to another city give this woman rest?

A man asked, "How long should I stay in my marriage when my wife does not share my faith and resists finding a faith of her own? Life has become a constant battle."

How would you answer this man? Is his wife's faith the real issue? What's the true cause of the power struggle in this marriage? If the man decides to leave will he find rest?

A young actress asked, "Is it really possible for a Christian to survive in the entertainment industry? Sometimes I feel like giving up and going back to being a secretary!"

Will this woman find any more rest from the conflict between her faith and the moral values of people around her back in Baltimore working as a secretary than as an aspiring actress in Hollywood?

A man in San Diego wrote to me, "When is it okay to leave a church that is no longer satisfying your spiritual need? I want some rest from the problems in my church!"

Is there a church that can assure this man rest from challenges? Would this be true rest?

Another man asked, "When are difficulties a sign that the Lord wants you to do something else? Are problems a sign that you should be where you are or guidance that you should move on?"

All these people are experiencing the longing to escape. Is this universal longing wrong?

In *Travels with Charley: In Search of America,* John Steinbeck tells about his journey all over the United States with his dog Charley. Wherever Steinbeck went he met people who envied his carefree travels. Steinbeck says he saw in people's eyes the longing "to get away, to move about, free and unanchored, not toward something but away from something."

One of my favorite conversations in the book is between Steinbeck and a storekeeper. Looking at Steinbeck's trailer the storekeeper asked, "You going in that?"

"Sure," Steinbeck responded.

"Where?" the man wanted to know.

"All over," the author said.

Then Steinbeck commented on this exchange. He wrote, "I saw what I was to see so many times on the journey—a look of longing. 'Lord, I wish I could go!' 'Don't you like it here?' 'Sure.

It's all right, but I wish I could go' 'You don't even know where I'm going.' 'I don't care. I'd like to go anywhere.'"[1]

The Yen to . . .

We've all had this yen. Sometimes it's just a desire to travel and see different places. Other times it's a desire to escape reality or responsibilities. The Bible does tell us the Lord provides a way of escape when we are tempted (1 Cor. 10:13). However, He does not provide easy escapes from duties He's assigned to us or from relationships or places in which He's deployed us.

The issue for us is prayerfully to seek the Lord's guidance to know where He wants us to be and what He wants us to do. The only acceptable reason to move to another place or situation is because of a greater opportunity to serve Him, not simply to escape present tensions or difficulties.

This chapter is for those who are where God wants them to be, yet they are experiencing stressful burdens in the midst of their faithfulness and sometimes wish they could escape. I want to emphasize that our Lord has promised us rest for those times when we become restless. An easy, problem-free life is not a sure sign we are in the Lord's will. Instead, when we face our difficulties through His power, we experience an incredible inner peace while storms of difficulty, conflict, and misunderstanding thunder around us.

Consistently, on time, and in time, for our most stressful times, the Lord sends a rainbow as a sign of His covenant with us.

A Rainbow Promise for Times of Stress

Christ's rainbow "I will" promise for times of stress is "I will give you rest" (Matt. 11:28). Here is the antidote to escapism, the cure for restlessness.

Often when I ask Christians how they are doing, they respond, "Just hanging in there." Christ's promise provides more than this kind of passive "What else can I do?" attitude. Christ wants to give us courage to hang tough when the going is rough.

Christ's rest is not a sleepy quietude. It would be better to translate this "I will" promise as "I will refresh you" or "I will rejuvenate you." The Greek compound verb *anapauo* is in the causative active voice, *anapauso*. In the context of Christ's broader statement we see that His rest is a dynamic quality given to us as we "labor and are heavy laden." He says, "*I will give you* rest. Take My yoke upon you and learn from Me, for I am gentle and lowly in heart, and you *will find rest for your souls*. For My yoke is easy and My burden is light" (Matt. 11:28–30).

Note that we do not escape responsibility, but with Christ's rejuvenation, leadership, and strength we are able to carry out our responsibility with supernatural power and joy.

Rest for the Weary

Who are the weary and heavy-laden Christ called? I think He had in mind more than those who were bone tired from physical labor. Rather, I believe Christ's sublime call was to stressed religious, conscientious Jews who were trying to do all that was required to be right with God. The terms of this self-generated righteousness were delineated in the heavy burden of the rules and regulations of the scribes and Pharisees. The term "a thousand and one" comes from the number of these requirements, an Hebraism for "limitless number." The people were burdened trying to do what the fastidious leaders loaded onto them. Their load was legalism at its worst: works righteousness with a magnitude of minutia.

But how does Christ's promise speak to us today? The surface answer is that it applies to those Christians who are burdened down with the heavy load of trying to justify themselves by good works rather than living by faith. There is a brand of legalistic Christianity which piles upon striving believers not only the biblical mandates, but also, with equal zeal, human requirements and customs.

Going Deeper

Yet I'm convinced Christ's invitation is especially applicable to those of us who try to live our discipleship on our own strength. Sooner or later, we run out of human steam.

As the old phrase goes, "We get weary in well-doing." Or, we feel frustrated by trying to be faithful. The burdens of people's needs become crushing. The inner wells of spiritual strength get drained. We sense the "depowering" stress of trying to change people and stew in the juices of our exasperation when we can't get them to do or be what we want. And when others don't seem to share the burden of our vision—whether it's evangelism, mission, social reform, community action, political involvement, the abortion issue, sexuality, race and ethnic relations, or some church committee we lead—we often become frustrated and discouraged.

The Greater Burden

An even greater burden we carry is for the complex, complicated person inside us. We'd like to blame our stress on the people or situations the Lord has called us to care about, but actually the trouble lies deeper. The real cause of our restless moods and feelings is inside. Or rather, what's lacking inside.

We need abiding peace to be the kind of people who can minister to the brokenness in others and in the world around us.

And this deep inner peace is impossible without abundant spiritual resources—a daily, hourly replenishment by the Spirit of Christ.

Rejuvenation in the Yoke

This rest, rejuvenation, that Christ offers to those who labor, the replenishment that provides deep inner peace, is not given in lethargic ease, but within the yoke of Christ. His "I will" promise of rest is immediately followed by His secret of when and how this rejuvenation is given to us: "Take My yoke upon you and learn from Me, for I am gentle and lowly in heart, and you will find rest for your souls."

This verse changed my life when I really understood what Christ meant. It helped me grasp the interdependence Christ offers me. When I became a Christian I thought of my discipleship as *my* responsibility to *do* for Him. As the years passed and I became a husband, a father, a clergyperson, I felt burdened by the immense load of being a diligent disciple *for* Christ. And, yes, at times I did get physically tired and emotionally weary. But it wasn't the kind of drained exhaustion that's cured by a good night's sleep or a vacation away from it all.

Some of my friends were quick to give simple advice: "Give your burdens to the Lord and leave them with Him." Sounded wonderful. However, when I got up from my knees after prolonged prayers of commitment and surrender, there, staring me in the face, were the same duties of my calling to be faithful. There was no rest, no rejuvenation. How could I give my burdens to the Lord when they came from the very things I knew He had assigned me to do?

At a particularly dark, stormy time when problems were raining down on me, the Lord gave me this rainbow "I will" promise about His rejuvenation in *His* yoke. The splendor of this rainbow radiated the secret I'd missed. I was not to escape the duties of my life, family, and ministry. They were all a part of Christ's yoke, which He was willing to share with me.

When Christ invited us to share His yoke, He was speaking about the training yoke used to train young oxen. As a carpenter Christ surely had made many yokes. These training yokes had a smaller opening on one side for the head of the younger ox and a larger opening for the head of the other older, more experienced and stronger bovine. The yoke rested on the shoulders of both, but the weight of pulling a plow was born by the stronger, more mature ox.

Further, the training yoke taught the young ox to respond to the reins and to plow a straight furrow. The older ox led the way. The trainee could not pull away and go off in its own direction. If it tried, its neck would be rubbed raw.

God the Father gave Christ the yoke to be the reigning Lord of history, the church, and your life and mine. We never outgrow our need to be in the trainee's side of His yoke as He calls us to share His work in redeeming the world.

The Advantage of Christ's Yoke

We feel the pride of Jesus the carpenter and the vision of Christ the Savior when He says, "Take My yoke upon you and learn from *Me,* for I am gentle and lowly of heart, and you will find rest for your souls. For My yoke is easy and My burden is light." As a carpenter, Jesus made yokes that were smooth, without rough places to cause abrasions on the oxen's necks, or slivers that could make the load more painful.

As our Lord, Christ is careful to call us into a yoke with Him where the trainee's side is "easy." We should not be thrown off by the use of the English word "easy" to translate the Greek word in the original text. It is *chrestos,* which means, "fit for use, able to be used and therefore good." It also means "kindly" or "gracious." Easy does not mean that it requires no effort on our part. However, the great advantage of Christ's yoke is we are in it with Him. He pulls the load; our challenge is to trust His lifting, pulling strength and keep pace with Him. He alone can help us walk with Him toward His destination for us. And all along the way He is kind and gracious to provide us with exactly what we need.

What We Learn in Christ's Yoke

Familiarity with this "I will" promise of Christ should not keep us from a fresh amazement over what He offers to teach us in His yoke. "Learn from Me, for I am gentle and lowly of heart."

Here the Greek word for "gentle" is *praus*. In this context it means "leadable, responsive to the reins." And the word for "lowly" is *tapeinos*, meaning "humble, receptive, open to be led, to grow, teachable."

In His incarnate life, Jesus revealed those qualities in their maximum meaning. As preexistent Logos, equal with the Father, He humbled Himself and was sent by the Father to be our Savior. From the human side of His divine-human nature, we behold what gentleness and humility really are. Jesus constantly told people He had come not to do His own will but the will of the Father. He showed us the true power of obedience. And Christ modeled for us what it means to be a servant. From Him we learn to trust God completely, wait for His timing, and expect His miracles.

At the end of His incarnate ministry on earth, Christ gave us His last will and testament. It incorporated all that He had come to earth to do in His exemplary life, His epicenter message about new life in the kingdom of God, and His expiatory death for our sins. Jesus said, "Peace I leave with you, My peace I give to you; not as the world gives do I give to you. Let not your heart be troubled, neither let it be afraid" (John 14:27). Don't miss the emphasis on *My*. Nothing less than the peace we see throughout Christ's life is offered to us.

In our relationship with the living Christ, He wants to reproduce His nature in ours, His gentleness and humility, so we can experience His rest. It simply means doing what He has called us to do, yoked with Him, with His strength, His guidance, His pacing, and for His glory.

Light Burdens

The result of a consistent life in the yoke with Christ, constantly receiving His rest, is offered in the last phrase of this rainbow "I will" promise: "My burden is light."

There are two words in Greek that are used for burden. One is *baros,* which means a weight that presses on us physically. The other is *phortion,* something to be carried; it is used metaphorically (with only one exception for the lading of a ship—Acts 27:10) for tasks, opportunities, and duties we assume. *Phortion* is used to translate Jesus's Aramaic word in the phrase "My burden is light." The best English translation for this kind of burden could be "responsibility."

For example, I can say that I have a burden to write this book to share what the Lord helped me discover about His covenant faithfulness displayed in His rainbows in the rain and what I've learned about claiming His "I will" promises while making each promise our own. It is a *phortion* kind of burden; I want to do this because the Lord clearly guided me to do it. But it could become a *baros* burden if I didn't depend on Christ's pulling, inspiring, uplifting power from His side of the yoke as I write each paragraph.

The same is true of all of life. Anything eventually becomes a drudgery if we try to do it on our own strength. But even the most mundane task can become a delight when we do it with gentleness and humility, leadability, and receptivity, when we are yoked with Christ. This is especially true for our calling to be servants in caring for others.

The apostle Paul makes this clear in Galatians 6:2–5, where he uses both *baros* and *phortion* in a fascinating way. "Bear one another's burdens, and so fulfill the law of Christ. For if anyone thinks himself to be something, when he is nothing, he deceives himself. But let each one examine his own work, and then he will have rejoicing in himself alone, and not in another. For each one shall bear his own load."

In verse 2, the Greek word for "burdens" is *bare,* the plural of *baros,* while in verse five, the word for "load" is *phortion.* The apostle calls all Christians to assume the responsibility of their calling to help others bear their physical or psychological burdens that have been placed on them by life. This *phortion* to care for others is a vital aspect of life in the yoke of Christ. We join Him in the work and He gives us the strength and wisdom to do it.

Life with a New Perspective

Christ's "I will" promise of His rejuvenation changes our perspective on the responsibilities from which we sometimes long to escape. And there is no "exit" sign along the corridors of life. The only lasting joy is to be where Christ wants us.

And the reward? Nonstop rejuvenation when we need it most. Rest. Christ's peace. Life in His yoke. Who would want to be anywhere else?

7

Christ's Amazing Confidence in Us

Follow Me, and I will make you fishers of men.

Matthew 4:19

*I*t *is* amazing.

The confidence Christ has in us.

In the previous chapter we talked about the confidence we can place in Him to give us a steady flow of rejuvenation while we are yoked with Him. And yet, we can't shake the amazement we feel that He would even call us, entrust great responsibilities to us, and desire to work through us to get His work done in the world.

There's a tremendous difference between self-confidence and Christ-confidence. The first can produce arrogance; the second provides a wonderful assurance. Self-confidence is limited to what we can produce on our own limited strength and ability. Christ-confidence has no limits because it's based on our willingness multiplied by His infinite willingness. Self-confidence eventually will bring us to a realization of our inadequacies and make us cowards where we could count. Christ-confidence makes us bold.

When We Need Christ-Confidence

The time we need Christ-confidence the most is when we have an opportunity to witness for Him. Few things can cloud our skies more than our tongue-tied reluctance to share Christ with someone who desperately needs His love and hope. The clouds become darker and the thunder rumbles when we see how secretive we are about our faith. Often our commitment to Christ is a

113

private affair. Frequently we are reticent to take a strong stand on what we believe in moral and social issues.

Why is it so difficult for many Christians to talk naturally and effectively about their faith? Social pressure, the fear of rejection, the quest for success? Or could it be that we've had bad experiences with glib Christians? Or perhaps it's our own lack of clarity about our faith that makes us timid.

Whatever the cause, eventually the Christian life becomes one long, dull rainy afternoon when we consistently resist communicating Christ to others. I often meet Christians whose faith has reached a plateau of boredom and blandness because they are not involved in the exciting adventure of introducing people to Christ. But I've also discovered that guilt-produced "oughts" about personal evangelism and social responsibility do not end the rains of passive resistance. Rather, it's Christ's amazing confidence in us that overcomes our lack of confidence in ourselves. And you guessed it: This confidence is expressed in some magnificent rainbows in the rain.

Three "I Will" Rainbows

There are three confidence-building "I will" rainbow promises of Christ. The first one defines the call of every Christian; the second reveals the source of our effectiveness in our calling; and the third offers the ultimate reward of accepting our calling.

People Fishers

The first "I will" promise that is power-packed with the intentionality of the Master is "Follow Me, and I will make you fishers of men" (Matt. 4:19). This invitation was first given by Jesus at the beginning of His ministry. In Luke's version it is, "Do not be afraid. From now on you will catch men" (Luke

5:10). It's important to note that Jesus was talking about a particular kind of fishing in which fish were still alive when they were caught and brought to shore. The Greek verb used to translate Jesus' Aramaic word for "catch" is *zogreo,* meaning "to catch alive" or "to take alive." "Follow Me" Jesus says to every Christian, "and I will empower you to take people alive." The obvious implication is that we are to communicate the delight of life in Christ gently and graciously rather than gaffing people with guilt or spearing them to death with secondary rules and regulations. Christ needs witnesses who are not "kill-joys" but examples of the authentic joy only He can give. This requires sharing the joy that Christ has produced in our lives.

Joy is the outward manifestation of grace. Sharing our joy leads to talking about its source in the unqualified giving and forgiving love of God in Christ. In the most natural way, we can talk about what the grace of Christ's cross and reconciliation did for us while we were separated from God by our sins. We can share what our brand of sin was without either doting on it or gloating over it. Our main thrust is to communicate the difference in our life after we committed our lives to Christ and were filled with His joy.

This kind of people-fishing is done in the context of caring friendships in which others feel our affirmation of them and our empathy for their needs and problems. Be sure of this: If we commit to establishing deep relationships, serving people, and being willing to talk about our faith in Christ, we'll be in the people-fishing business. We'll have more opportunities to introduce people to Christ than we ever imagined possible.

Jean the Fisher

My friend Jean is this kind of fisher. She has claimed Christ's promise to make her a fisher of people. She is an attractive disciple of Christ who radiates His love and sparkles with His joy. After coming alive through a recommitment of her own life to Christ, she became a conscientious student of the Bible and was constantly alert for opportunities to share her faith with her friends. She became an effective, winsome witness for Christ.

However, Jean's deepest concern was for her Jewish husband, Sam. With sustaining Christ-confidence, she prayed without ceasing for him, never pushing, but constantly seeking to reveal what a difference Christ made in her life. Often Sam came to worship with Jean. I sensed she was praying for him throughout the sermons. She longed for Sam to know Christ as his Messiah, to experience true *shalom*.

One day, both of them came to see me. Sam was facing a serious operation and wanted me to pray for him. This was an opportunity to talk about his relationship to Christ. He indicated his openness and, with Jean quietly praying at his side, I prayed that Christ would be with Sam through the operation and that he would receive the gift of faith to trust Christ completely with his whole life. Jean had already shared with Sam the steps to full salvation, so my task as a friend was simply to affirm the clear, biblical truths she had communicated.

Sometime after Sam's operation and recovery, he suffered a vision problem. His seeing was clouded and he couldn't see clearly even at a short distance. One evening while they were watching television the screen became totally blurred to Sam. He left the den and went into their living room and stretched out on the couch, unable to see across the room. Then he prayed, "Father, send Your Son to heal my eyes." When Sam opened his eyes, he could see across the room with perfect clarity.

The next day Sam burst into my office with the exciting news. He told me what happened to his eyes, but also what happened in his mind and heart. "Lloyd," he said with a beaming countenance, "I'm a Christian. Christ is my Messiah!"

When Sam made his confession of faith before the officers of our church and became a member, it was wonderful to sense the Christ-shalom of a completed Jew. Now the questioning, searching, wondering look on his face was replaced with sheer joy that sparkled and flowed from Christ's grace in his heart. I couldn't help praying a prayer inside as Sam spoke. "Thank You, Lord, that You used fisher Jean to catch Sam."

And the best news is that now Sam and Jean are in the people-fishing business together. I'm thankful for the impact of their leadership in our church as well as the impact of their influence among their friends and in the community.

The Ecstasy of People-Fishing

Looking back over many years of ministry, I can say that my most thrilling moments have been when I see church members succeed at people-fishing. I know firsthand the ecstasy of catching people for Christ, and I want it for every Christian. I sense what it does for their faith as they experience Christ-confidence. There's nothing more satisfying and fulfilling than being a part of the ultimate miracle of the transformation of a person into a new creature, destined to live now and forever! So if your life has had the continuous dull feeling of a stormy, rainy period without a break, there is a rainbow for you—"I will make you fishers of people!"

Christ's Confidence

Throughout the Gospels we are amazed by Christ's confidence in the disciples—and us. He entrusts the future expansion of the kingdom to us. We are His strategy for changing the world. Even when He shifts the metaphor from fish to vines and branches, the same confidence is expressed: "You did not choose Me, but I chose and appointed you that you should go and bear fruit, and that your fruit should remain" (John 15:16). Strange confidence, indeed, for the likes of some of us.

It is an astounding thing, isn't it? It startles the mind, stirs the soul. Before we chose to respond, Christ chose us; before we even desired to know Him, Christ desired us. It is an affirming, encouraging assurance that Christ wants us to be with Him. "Now there's a man . . . there's a woman . . . I'd like to have with Me," He says about us. "There's the kind of person who, when totally committed to Me and filled with My Spirit, can be My witness, can show the world what abundant living in Me is all about."

Christ has a quadrifocal focus of His vision of us. Yes, He can see the person we've been and He sees what we are most of the time. But He also sees the person He can make us and the part we can play in sharing His love.

But we shouldn't be surprised. After all, look at the kinds of people Christ chose to be His disciples, followers, and friends. Few could have passed a contemporary headhunter's scrutiny for a movement to change the world. Not many would have passed muster for a pulpit nominating committee today or been on the list of nominees for church officership. But Christ chose them because He both liked and loved them, enjoyed being with them, and knew what they could become.

And now He has chosen us. Did He make a mistake in judgment? No. He keeps calling people like you and me because He wants to display what He can do with needy people. Paul was right, "We have this treasure in earthen vessels, that the excellence of the power may be of God and not of us" (2 Cor. 4:7). This is the corrective: We do not witness to our excellence as part of our candidacy for discipleship, but rather the excellency of the Lord's power to remake women and men like us.

It's what we've been through and, yes, even what we are going through that makes us effective witnesses for Christ. Our words are authentic when we say to someone, "I understand what you're going through," or "I really know how you're feeling." This authenticity gives us the right to listen and then to respond with a sensitive sharing of what new life in Christ can mean.

Go Share Life

There are two verses in Acts that I use to keep me focused in my essential calling to share Christ's life-transforming power. The first is Acts 4:13: "When they saw the boldness of Peter and John, and perceived that they were uneducated and untrained men, they marveled. And they realized that they had been with Jesus." The other verse is Acts 5:20—Christ's reiterated call through an angel when the apostles were miraculously released from prison—"Go, stand in the temple and speak all the words of this life." Or, as the New English Bible renders it, "Go . . . and tell the people all about this new life."

What our world needs are ordinary people who have made time with the Lord their most crucial priority. I want to be one of these people because I know time alone with Christ provides the fresh power, love, and joy that gives me what people really need. And it's with Christ I am free of any artificiality or dependence on human skill or cleverness. When I am honest with Him, I can be real with people. Then I can follow the admonition, "Tell the people all about this new life."

We are all experts at one thing: what it has meant for us to meet Christ, grow in the new life in Him, grapple with the soul-sized issues of life with Him, receive the answers for our toughest questions from Him, and experience fresh anointing of power of the Spirit through Him. This is the expertise necessary to meet people where they are with empathy and hope. If we lack expertise, then our first step in fishing for people is to get expertise through our own relationship with the Savior. Are we living a life with Him that we would want everyone to experience? Is our own faith exciting? If not, why not?

But What Will I Say?

Even with this assurance our vision of being Christ's fishers of people becomes cloudy with self-doubt over whether we will know what to say when we are confronted with people's questions, arguments, or complex problems. For this insecurity Christ gives us a second "I will" promise. It was given to the disciples for tough times of examination or trial because of their faith in Him. The promise is applicable whenever we take a stand for Him or in any challenging exchange with a troubled person. Whatever the case, Christ promises, "It will turn out for you as an occasion for testimony. Therefore settle it in your hearts not to meditate beforehand on what you will answer; for I *will give you a mouth and wisdom* which all your adversaries will not be able to contradict or resist" (Luke 21:13–15).

I know this promise works. Through the years I have found Christ faithful to keep this promise. Repeatedly I have experienced the twin gifts of wisdom and words to probe to the real issues a person was facing then respond with inspired insight I knew the Lord gave me. It happens when I pray constantly while talking with a person about his or her faith or some deep question or problem. There is no way that we can assemble pat answers for every type of person or need.

Good thing. They would have a hollow ring and be putoffs or putdowns. Of course, we draw on our study of the Scriptures, the insights of great Christian thinkers of the ages, the refinement of our own understanding of tough theological issues, and a careful observation of the human personality. But it is the Spirit who guides us moment by moment in what to ask and what to say. Our basic purpose is to help a person to meet Christ. He wants this even more than we do, so we can proceed with confidence. If we are careful to give Him the glory, He will use us.

A Third Rainbow and a Warning

The third "I will" rainbow about our calling to be witnesses provides us with an ultimate confidence or an urgent concern. From it we learn what Christ will do for those who become willing and effective communicators of their faith in Him, taking a bold stand for Him in moral, spiritual, and social issues, and what He will not do for those who refuse. The first part gives us a great assurance, the second part a cause for alarm. "Therefore whoever confesses *Me* before men, him I will confess before My Father who is in heaven. But whoever denies *Me* before men, him I will also deny before My Father who is in heaven" (Matt. 10:32–33, italics added).

The Aramaic idiom Christ used, when reproduced in the Greek, really means "confess *in* me," indicating unity with Him and the person who takes his or her courageous stand for Him publicly. What is meant is not a once-done, glib, verbal gymnastic expressed while joining the church, but to make known in every relationship that we are a woman or a man who lives in Christ and in whom He lives.

The amazing confidence we gain from being a faithful witness is that Christ will confess His union with us to the Father, both now and at the point of our physical death. Christ will attest that we belong to Him and have not been ashamed to have everyone know it.

The flip side is that those who willfully remain silent about their closet Christianity will not be attested to by Christ. A silent Christian is guilty of denial as much as a person who makes no pretense of believing in Christ, or flat-out rejects Him.

What shall we do with this disturbing word from the Lord? There's only one thing we can do with it: Accept the warning as it stands. The salient truth is that anyone who consistently denies the opportunity to share Christ's love and help others know Him would be very uncomfortable in heaven anyway. The main activity in heaven is proclaiming the glory of God and cheering on the expansion of His kingdom on earth.

If in Heaven, Why Not Now?

Last World Communion Sunday, I felt led to preach a communion meditation on "If in Heaven, Why Not Now?" I described John's vision of heaven in Revelation 7:9–10:

> After these things I looked, and behold, a great multitude which no one could number, of all nations, tribes, peoples, and tongues, standing before the throne and before the Lamb, clothed with white robes, with palm branches in their hands, and crying out with a loud voice, saying, "Salvation belongs to our God who sits on the throne, and to the Lamb!"

The message was particularly pointed for a church at the center of the Los Angeles basin, just five months after the riots the previous spring. These riots, and the subsequent burning and looting, were a wakeup call to a city that had neglected for too long its strained ethnic conflict, the employment and housing problems of the disadvantaged, and the lack of confidence in police enforcement. Our church was actively involved in feeding and clothing the victims in the riot's aftermath and many members took leading roles in rebuilding the city.

Now, on World Communion Sunday, it was time to affirm our oneness in Christ within our multi-ethnic, multi-cultural congregation. If heaven was going to be one continuous praise to God by all races, our church was to be a foretaste of heaven. We had to confess our unity in Christ and make a commitment to bring to our city the racial harmony we were experiencing in our church.

Before taking Communion, we confessed our sins of neglect and any vestige of prejudice or judgment possibly lingering in our hearts. And then, from roving microphones all over our large sanctuary, we heard people pray in their native tongues—more than twenty different dialects from Asia, Africa, Europe, Mexico, and South America—prayers confessing Christ as Lord and interceding for our city.

When I broke the Bread and raised the Cup before Communion, I felt led to ask people from various ethnic groups to come forward to assist me: African-Americans, Asian-Americans, Hispanics, and Caucasians. After breaking the Bread, symbolic of Christ's broken body, African-Americans and Koreans, representing groups so often at odds with each other in our city, fed each other, saying, "Christ's body was broken for you and me so that our brokenness might be healed."

Then I asked one person from each of the major ethnic groups to place his or her hand on the Communion chalice and join me in raising it before the people. The congregation sat stunned, then broke forth in singing, "He is Lord, He is risen from the dead and *He* is Lord. Every knee shall bow and every tongue confess that Jesus Christ is Lord!"

As moving as this foretaste of heaven was, we all knew it would have lasting authenticity only if each of us confessed Christ as Lord to people regardless of their ethnic background, as well as work for justice in the exposed, unhealed, tensions in our city.

Many of our people who had remained silent in social gatherings when racial slurs were expressed now had to speak out.

Business leaders had to put their faith into action and take a stand. And the unrighteous leaven of prejudice in all of our hearts had to be purged.

Somehow, the picture of what we will do in heaven became a sharp contrast to what we weren't doing on earth, in our city, in our neighborhoods, and at our places of work.

Do We Want to Go to Him?

So the second part of Christ's rainbow promise about confessing Him before others confronts us with the question of whether we really want to go to heaven. We'll all live forever; the question is, Where? If our faith means so little to us that we bypass opportunities to share Christ and work under the plumb line of His justice and righteousness in all of society, it may expose the truth that we're not very concerned about whether we will spend eternity in heaven or not.

But I suspect that for you this is not even a tolerable alternative. So say I! We want to live, speak, and act out our life in Christ and live with the amazing confidence He has placed in us. And what a joy it is even now to hear Him say, "Father, this person is one of My cherished, called, and empowered witnesses. I like and love him/her. It's a delight to count her/him as one of My disciples . . . a courageous communicator, a bold witness living in the joy of Our rainbow covenant. Bless him/her now and when it's time to make physical death a transition to the next phase of the glory of heaven We know together. This is one I want to be with *Us* forever!"

With an amazing confidence like this from Christ, I don't want to disappoint Him. How about you?

The Rainbow That Touches the Graveyard

And I, if I am lifted up from earth, will draw all peoples to
Myself.

John 12:32

W hat I'm about to share with you may sound fanciful and contrived. It's neither. It really happened.

The reason it was so special to me, so confirming of the desire to write this book, was that it happened while I was preparing to write this particular chapter on Christ's "I will" promise, "And I, if I am lifted up from earth, will draw all peoples to Myself" (John 12:32).

I was seated at a desk in my hotel room in Edinburgh. The desk was in front of a window that looks out over the city. Immediately across the street below is St. Cuthbert's Church and its historic graveyard.

It had been storming and raining heavily all afternoon, which made it a good time to be indoors studying my Bible, opened to John 12, with an array of commentaries and books on the cross and the new covenant. Next to these were stacks of letters I had received during the previous year in which people confided their aching needs.

Late in the afternoon, I realized that the rain was no longer spattering against the window pane. I looked up and saw that the storm was subsiding. And there in the sky was a magnificent rainbow. Its colors were breathtaking—red, purple, blue, yellow, and green.

Now, I've already shared with you other rainbows I saw that summer in Scotland. This one, however, was even more perfectly timed. More important to me was the way the rainbow was positioned in the sky.

Picture it in your mind's eye as I remember this rainbow—one end of it reached into the remaining clouds in the sky while the arched splendor of the other end extended right down into St. Cuthbert's graveyard across the street!

I was stunned. The multicolored rays of the rainbow bathed the trees. They danced on the grim, gray surfaces of the monuments in the graveyard!

Unable to contain my excitement, I splurged and called home. With the time difference, my wife Mary Jane was just starting her day. As I described the incredible sight she quickly responded to the delight I was feeling. I did my best to put into words the breathtaking extravaganza of nature I was beholding.

"Think of it!" I exclaimed. "At the very time I'm sitting here praying about the rainbow as the sign of the covenant, here is the most spectacular natural rainbow I've ever seen!"

"How amazing!" Mary Jane said enthusiastically. "I can't see it, but I sure can feel what it's doing for you. Lloyd, it's no coincidence that rainbow is happening at this moment. The Lord is trying to tell you something."

I'm glad she said it. I had not dared to assume that the Lord had arranged the atmospheric conditions for this rainbow just for me. A surge of awe swept over me as I felt an inner confirmation that her intuition was right. Whatever else the Lord was up to with this beautiful rainbow, He certainly used it in my life that afternoon.

Another Rainbow That Reaches the Graveyard

I was transfixed by the rainbow until it slowly vanished. Only then could I reflect on what the Lord might have been seeking to communicate to me. I could not get off my mind the lasting impression of the way its rays had splashed so brilliantly on the graves.

Then I understood. Christ, the rainbow of the new covenant, reaches down to the graveyards of the living dead. It is the magnificent power of the crucified Lord who can raise those who are dead spiritually, buried in the graves of their own or life's making. Only the voice from the cross can raise the morally or intellectually dead. Nothing less than His voice can say, "Come forth" to those being buried alive by Satan. His rainbow is resplendent with the colors of purple and red—His shed blood and the redeeming passion. It is His cross that plummets to the depths of human shame and loss. Calvary is the only power that can wake up the aimless and stir the conscience of those who think they are blameless. The magnetism of the suffering Savior who prayed as He was impaled on the cross, "Father, forgive them," has the authority and the power to exhume our old selves from the graves. The Christ of the cross raids the graveyards of life. His rainbow splashes its glory on the gravestones that bear the date when Satan thought he had buried us with the dirt of either humanistic arrogance, intellectual pride, or determined self-justification.

So it is from this side of Calvary that we hear the voice of the Crucified, "Now is the judgment of this world; now the ruler of this world will be cast out. And I, if I am lifted up from the earth, will draw all peoples to Myself" (John 12:31–32). This astounding rainbow assurance is a matter of life and death, a further application of a previous promise, "Most assuredly, I say to you, he who hears My word and believes in Him who sent Me has everlasting life, and shall not come into judgment, but has passed from death into life. . . . the hour is coming, and now is, when the dead will hear the voice of the Son of God; and those who hear will live" (John 5:24–25).

The Graveyard of "All Peoples"

The promise "I will draw all peoples to Myself" expresses Christ's inclusive vision of His drawing, uplifting, magnetic power as the only Savior of all nations and races throughout all of human history. The assertion was given on the heels of what happened in Jerusalem that day during His last week of incarnate ministry.

Some Greek proselytes to the Hebrew religion came from Greece to the Holy City for Passover. They were interested in Jesus and wanted a private audience with Him. "Sir, we wish to see Jesus," they told Philip, who then shared the request with Andrew. Together they told Jesus, probably thinking this was the beginning of the Master's impact on the kingdoms of the world.

Jesus was ready for this possibility for human glory. He had encountered before this beguiling temptation to avoid the cross. In the wilderness Satan had tried the strategy to distract Jesus from His greater purpose. The account of the temptation from Luke 4:1–13 reminds us that Satan took Jesus up on a high mountain and showed Him all the kingdoms of the world "in a moment of time." The devil said to Him, "All this authority I will give You, and their glory; for this has been delivered to me, and I give it to whomever I wish. Therefore, if You will worship before me, all will be Yours." Jesus's answer was decisive: "Get behind Me, Satan! For it is written, 'You shall worship the LORD your God, and Him only you shall serve.'" Luke comments, "Now when the devil had ended every temptation, he departed from Him until an opportune time."

After this earlier confrontation with Satan, Jesus was prepared for any additional distractions. Because of this, Jesus' response to the requests from the Greeks might seem unresponsive to a great opportunity to influence Greece through these potential disciples. I think Jesus saw it as another temptation to be the temporal leader of the kingdoms of the world. Jesus was not an opportunist. He knew He could gain the acclaim of all nations as the greatest political personage of history, living a long physical life to old age.

However, Jesus knew that it was not His destiny to be the most revered philosopher, scholar, or ruler of human kingdoms, but to be the Savior of the world. So His response to everyone around Him that day in Jerusalem was to reassert His true destiny: to glorify God by going to the cross. After the cross and resurrection and His glorification by God, He would reach the nations of the world. As the crucified and risen Savior and Lord, Jesus would draw all peoples to Himself.

This is exactly what has happened through the centuries. It's the magnetism of the cross that draws people to Christ, and through Him to the Father. As we've said repeatedly, the cross is the Father's reach across the breach of our separation from Him with His own shed blood and broken body. Christ forged the new covenant. And now He continues confronting the life-or-death issue of those living in the graveyards. He answers the Father's question to Ezekiel, "Son of man, can these bones live?" Jesus is the one who proclaims with divine authority and with the power of the cross: "O dry bones, hear the word of the LORD! . . . Surely I will cause breath to enter into you, and you shall live" (Ezek. 37:3–5). Christ, the rainbow, reaches the graves with life.

What's Dead or Dying in Us

Unfortunately, the spiritual graveyards of the world contain not only agnostics, but also Christians—sometimes people like you and me. Often we remain in graves from which we need the magnetic Savior to draw us.

As I mentioned previously, on my desk in my room in Edinburgh, mingled with my Bible, books, and writing pad, were some of the letters I received throughout the year from people in my congregation and the radio and television audience. Beside my chair was a trunk filled with hundreds more. As I re-read those letters throughout my study leave, I became acutely aware of the graves of remorse, fear, anxiety, worry, loneliness, and panic in which we live at times. We all have occasions when our faith, joy, and passion are not as vibrantly alive as they were when we were first drawn to the Lord. And we all know church people who act like they never were truly alive in Christ. And who hasn't heard the ghastly words of negative prophesy of "a dying church"?

We are moved to pray in the stormy times of life, "Oh, Uplifted Crucified Lord, bring us all back to Your cross, draw us to Yourself, revive us, show us again Your nail-pierced hands, Your bleeding head and side, Your death for us. Melt our chilly hearts. We grow accustomed to a fraction of the abundant life You died for and now live to give us. When we forget, lead us to Calvary!"

That's one prayer the Lord always answers with His rainbow "I will" promise, only now it is spoken to us with second-person intensity, "When you come to Me by way of My cross, I will draw you to Myself."

How does He do it? Let's think about some of the temporary sloughs, pits, and open graves of the graveyard of life from which He extricates us so we can really live. Some I want to mention were expressed in those letters, others I hear about in conversations with people almost every day. Satan has tried to use them at one time or another with all of us. We all have a common need: We need consistent fresh experiences with our Savior, who died for us and is present to help us stay alive at the foot of His magnetic, uplifting, liberating cross.

The Slough of Self-Centeredness

Notice I didn't say the "sloth" of self-centeredness but the "slough" of it. Of course, self-centeredness causes the indolence and laziness of sloth, but I'm using the word *slough* because it's descriptive of a deeper level of self-centeredness. Deeper indeed. A slough is a deep bog filled with miry mud that often acts like quicksand if you step into it.

My wife, Mary Jane, can tell you about slipping into bogs. One day our friend Willie Forbes, the noted painter and taxidermist, took the two of us to a very remote little loch in the Highlands to fish for brown trout. Getting there was not easy. When we reached the end of the road we had to leave Willie's Landrover behind and hike through more than a mile of miry bogs. It was rough going as we stepped from one firm mound of earth to another, trying to avoid the bogs in between. Mary Jane's legs are a lot shorter than mine or Willie's, so it was understandable that she had a hard time keeping up with us.

Suddenly Mary Jane cried for help. I turned back to her. She had slipped into one of the bogs and was in up to her hips in the slimy mud. Willie and I pulled her out.

Willie cautioned with a smile in his voice, "You've got to watch oot for these bogs. The'r like sin—they'll suck you in and then doon." We laughed together about the metaphor Willie seemed to enjoy pointing out to a pastor and his wife.

What is not laughable is the slough of self-centeredness. It has a way of sucking us into inordinate concern for our own welfare, sinking us deeper into the mud of self-pity when things don't go our way, and into the slime of selfishness. We all know times when we have slipped into this spiritual bog. And we also know that it's impossible to get ourselves out without help. We'll keep sinking deeper, all the while blaming, criticizing, and complaining.

Some of us who call ourselves Christians never have been pulled out of the slough of self-centeredness. And some who were once out find it all too easy to slip back into the bog.

Only the crucified Savior has the pulling, lifting power to get us out of the slough of self-centeredness. Jesus does it through His cross and the cross He calls us to take up in following Him. Christ's love for us on the cross lifts the self and gives it a new focus. When we grasp how much suffering Christ endured for each of us, and with the gift of faith can say, "He died for me," His drawing power lifts us out of our miry bog of self-concentration. The old gospel hymn is not trite but true, "Love lifted me, love lifted me; when nothing else could help, love lifted me."

But this is only the beginning. As Christ's cross continues to rivet our attention, we hear His call to deny ourselves, take up our crosses and follow Him. As I often have written, denial of self is not the obliteration of self, but a yielding to the Lordship and leadership of Christ. It is the surrender of the self to be filled with the Spirit of Christ.

When people say, "I need to get myself out of the way!" I know what they mean, but I also know what they need. It is to let Christ fill that self with His love and power. Trying to get rid of self is to end up with greater concentration on oneself. A self-centered person is simply one who has not been loved adequately by others and must try to provide what is lacking by doting on himself or herself. But only Christ can love us as much as we need to be loved. And when we allow Him to do this we are set free to love, forgive, care, and serve others. The sacrificial love of Christ's cross not only lifts us but also leads us to live His commandment to love. We will talk a lot about this in the next chapter, but for now, remember that Christ's promise to draw us to Himself and His cross is a matter of life or death. And now, life in Him begins with a new birth with our new self filled with the Spirit and focused on Him and the needs of others.

The Pit of Pride

The magnetic Christ of the cross also lifts us out of the pit of pride. We tend to think of pride as the exaltation of the self; actually it's the limitation of the self. Pride sets a limit on what we can do and what we can accomplish. It also restricts the degree of forgiveness we can feel to what we can atone for ourselves.

When a person falsely takes credit for what he or she has allegedly done, pride not only debilitates giving glory to the Lord, but it blocks the vision of His greater plan. I think a sure sign that we are drawn to Christ and are alive in Him is when we are challenged to try something we cannot pull off without His supernatural power. The risen Christ is available to us to put our complete trust in Him and venture forward, attempting the humanly impossible assignments of expanding His kingdom.

Yet the greater depreciating result of false pride is our reluctance to confess our sins and to receive forgiveness. We have a scale: On one side is the load of our sins; on the other side is our effort to exonerate ourselves. The scales never balance until this other side has the cross placed on it. When it is, the scales don't just balance, they immediately are overloaded on the side of the cross.

Again, the issue is a matter of life or death. When Christ singled us out, we were dead spiritually. Paul reminded the Colossians that they were dead in their trespasses when Christ made them alive with Him by forgiving those trespasses. He then used two powerful images for the liberating power of the cross.

In the cities of Asia Minor, charge sheets listing the debts or misdemeanors held against a person were displayed publicly.

Vellum paper was used, but it could not absorb the ink. The two signs that the debts had been paid or the crimes were exonerated were when a sponge was used to wipe clean the vellum-paper charge list and a nail was driven through it. Now we can appreciate Paul's assurance of what Christ did for us on the cross: "Having forgiven you all trespasses, having wiped out the handwriting of requirements that was against us, which was contrary to us. And He has taken it out of the way, having nailed it to the cross" (Col. 2:13b–14).

We are keenly aware of this in our new life with Christ. However, as the years go by we assume responsibility for keeping our own charge lists against ourselves. And we think we can wipe them clean and drive in our own nails of exoneration. Pride limits the list to our little mistakes and it keeps off the list the big failures. And, equally serious, pride causes us to sneak around Golgotha, which leads to the spiritual death of compounded guilt.

Fortunately, the Crucified Savior will not leave us in the pit of pride. He keeps coming for us. He "breaks the power of cancelled sin" as Charles Wesley called it, and draws us near by giving us a fresh experience of His grace. A vital part of this drawing process is to anoint our imaginations with the next steps of the adventure He has planned for us. We are overcome with "wonder, love, and praise." And since praise is the antidote to pride, the more we praise our Lord the less danger there is of falling back into the pit of pride. The rainbow reaches the pits in the graveyards of life.

The Open Graves of Grief

Christ's rainbow promise "I will draw you to Myself" also reaches the open graves of our grief. I call them open graves because they represent the losses of life for which we still need

Christ's healing comfort and conciliation. These gaping, open graves contain both the caskets of loved ones and all the lost wish-dreams of our yesterdays. We find it excruciatingly painful to say good-bye to whomever or whatever, knowing life will never quite be the same again. There are diminutive deaths we endure when what we cherish or long for either doesn't last or never material-izes. There's real grief attached to being phased out of a job, going through the loss of a marriage, losing your savings in a poorly con-ceived investment, or facing a prolonged illness or the limitations of growing old.

Grief is like a badly broken bone: It takes a long time to heal. And this says some good things about us. We really care. Loved ones are important to us. Life is precious. We know the value of what we've accomplished or achieved with the Lord's blessing. Grief over our losses is wrong only when it creates a false security. The refusal to be healed of grief, whatever has caused it, keeps us from closure and receptivity to what Christ has ahead for us. Also, self-prolonged grief robs the people around us of the love Christ wants to give them through us.

For instance, a mother endlessly mourned the death of one of her daughters. After a couple of years, her other daughter said to her, "You know, Mom, I miss Jane too, but your obsessive grief is making you and the whole family miserable. Jane's in heaven, but don't forget you've got the rest of us. You act like we're not very important. We need you to start living again, Mom!"

The Crucified Christ is the eternal healer of grief. The cross is the only effective poultice to draw out the poison of grief from our hearts. Through Christ's death-defeating Calvary we know that physical death has lost its sting, the grave its touted victory. But it is the presence and inexplicable comfort of Christ Himself that heals our griefs. It's one of His greatest miracles.

Christ's rainbow splashes its brilliant hope on the open graves in our hearts. "It's time to move on," He says gently. "I need you for My work with the people of your life and I have plans that I've decided you and I can accomplish together." Life goes on—not standing beside the open grave, but with the living!

Mausoleums of Moods

The rainbow I saw that afternoon in Edinburgh also splashed on the stately limestone mausoleums of St. Cuthbert's graveyard. It made me think of all the moods that keep us imprisoned and not free to live life to the fullest. Some of them become habits. Whenever I trace my moods back to their deeper cause, I realize they are usually prompted by my need to punish myself or someone else. I see the same proclivity in most people.

Our gloomy or discouraged moods are often the result of our impatience with ourselves or somebody. "Why didn't you do better?" we ask ourselves. "How could you have said that? or done this? Or acted so stupidly?" A bad mood usually results from this kind of tongue-lashing of ourselves. Other times our moods are ways of expressing our disappointment to people for what they have or have not said or done. We express our pique with a mood that speaks our judgment louder than words. People get the point, but we're the ones who suffer most. Our life in Christ is put on hold for a time—often too long a time.

The same emotional channel through which our bad moods flow can also carry the flow of joyous good moods. There's no other reliable, indefatigable source of the artisan flow than in the crucified Christ of the cross. He alone has the power to judge us in a way that does not disintegrate us emotionally but gives us courage to face what's wrong, and at the same time be liberated with the joy of being forgiven. And He also relieves us of the self-assumed responsibility to set people in line by our punitive moods.

Christ draws us out of our bad moods to His cross. Once more we are overcome by the depth of His love for us. A mood of adoration and praise results. What's more, we know where to go when we're tempted to use our own moods to punish ourselves or others.

An Everyday Cross

Once I was browsing in a Christian bookstore that also sold ecclesiastical supplies. It had beautiful crosses for sanctuary chancels as well as smaller ones to be worn as part of the vestments of the clergy. While I was browsing in the book stacks a woman came into the store and said, "I want a cross."

The clerk said, "This way, Madame," and led the woman to a counter where he had all sorts of crosses for communion tables and for wearing by the clergy.

The woman objected, "Oh, no, I want an everyday kind of cross."

What the woman wanted was a piece of jewelry to put around her neck. The adjective "everyday" modified the cross. I suspected what she needed—and what we all need—is an everyday cross, a daily experience of the Crucified Lord who promises, "Through the cross I will draw you to Myself." And this is what He does. Every day. Right now.

I Will Always Love You

He who has My commandments and keeps them, it is he who
loves Me. And he who loves Me will be loved by My Father,
and I will love Him and manifest Myself to him.

John 14:21

The little boy was sobbing uncontrollably. He kept hollering between each sob, "I want my dad!"

All the efforts of the baby-sitter to console the lad were to no avail. She had lost control. No wonder. She had tried to manage the boy by telling him that if he didn't do what she said, his father wouldn't love him anymore.

When the youngster's sobbing reached panic proportions, the baby-sitter finally called his parents. The parents rushed home and burst through the door. The father ran to his son, who stood in his pajamas in the middle of the living room, still hollering, "I want my dad!"

The father swooped the boy up in his arms and held him closely, repeating, "It's okay. Your dad's here now." Soon the son calmed down enough for his dad to ask what was wrong. With that, the boy began to wail again. He pointed to the baby-sitter.

"She said . . . (sob) . . . that if I didn't do what she said . . . (deep breath) . . . that you'd stop loving me!"

"Son, that's not true," his dad said tenderly. "I will always love you." He carried his son upstairs to his room repeating the words over and over again. The father continued repeating the reassurance until the lad fell asleep.

They did not hire that baby-sitter again.

Five Wonderful Words

Wonderful words: "I will always love you." We never outgrow the need to hear them. When we're good and not so good, when we fail and life goes bump, when we do stupid things and we test people's endurance.

We need these words from parents as long as they live and from memory's sacred treasure chest after they've died. The words are essential for a great marriage. We long for friends who can say these words. And they should be both spoken and experienced between church members.

"Always" covers a lot of territory. It spans the full spectrum of what we do and say and extends to the difficulties, problems, personality proclivities, frustrations, differences of will, conflicts, and misunderstandings in our relationships. It's quite a promise to say to anyone—child, parent, spouse, friend, or fellow believer—"I will always love you." Can we really say and mean this?

Too often we communicate just the opposite. There's an implied limit to our love. A veiled quid pro quo, a barter of approval or affirmation for performance we desire from another person. In most relationships there's a subtle (and sometimes not so subtle) demarcation line beyond which our love will not reach.

And even the best communicators of the faith, both clergy and laity, have a hard time presenting the grace and expectations of the Lord without coming across like a baby-sitter: "If you don't do what I say, the Lord will stop loving you."

It's a big challenge to talk about the judgment of the Lord or His unequivocal admonitions without getting our own qualified love demands mixed in so that we imply that God will "take away" just as we do. Many people are so conditioned by their background and culture that they project onto the Lord what they have experienced in human relationships: that their behavior determines how much He will love them. What is often lacking in preaching and teaching, as well as our sharing of what we believe, is that the Lord's judgment is an expression of His unqualified love and His desire for His best for us.

Added to this is our tendency to equate the mixed stew of problems, frustrations, and disappointments that life dishes out with a lack of Lord's love for us. Projecting our own bad relational habits onto Him, we entertain the assumption that we must have done something to alter His love for a time until we get back in line.

But what really causes our lives to be filled with a seemingly endless storm is our inability to say to the Lord, "I will always love You." This can happen when circumstances overpower us with the false idea that He has stopped loving us. It also happens when we are confronted with the awesome demands of being faithful in our love to Him.

You may expect me to say at this point, "Not to worry! It's not important how we love the Lord, but just keep emphasizing how much He loves us." I'm not going to say that because it will keep us from one of Christ's most brilliant "I will" rainbows. At first, it may sound like an offer of qualified love. The big "if" implied at the beginning of it might lead us to say, "You see, Christ does put a hefty qualification for receiving His and the Father's love. So if I don't measure up there's no way He's going to say, 'I will always love you.'"

And yet, when we understand this liberating rainbow in its context and as the climax of the five other "I wills" of Christ in the same passage, I think we'll see that what looks like qualified love is really an offer from Christ to give us the ability to receive. The condition presupposes that we have allowed Him to make us willing to receive what He wants to give us.

Here's the rainbow: "He who has My commandments and keeps them, it is he who loves Me. And he who loves Me will be loved by My Father, and *I will love him and manifest Myself to him*" (John 14:21, italics added).

This promise was given as a part of Jesus' message to His frightened disciples on the night before His crucifixion. If ever a group of people needed a rainbow to end a storm of doubt about the grace and goodness of God, these disciples did. They were burdened by an inexplicable grief. The cross loomed as an inevitable reality. Jesus would be taken away from them. The most loving, caring person they'd ever known was about to be executed.

Jesus knew what they were thinking and feeling. What would happen to the mission to which He had called them? How could they be faithful disciples without His commanding, towering, courage-instilling presence with them? How could they face the dangers ahead? They sensed a terrible emptiness, a greater panic than they had ever experienced, a gripping fear for what the future held without the Master.

The future also was on Christ's mind. Out of incomparable love for His disciples He had to impress on them the magnificent things that would happen to them after His cross and resurrection. Powerfully, He met each of the aching questions on the disciples hearts with five awesome "I will" promises, all building up to the sixth, the assurance expressing, "I will always love you."

Six Parts of One Great Rainbow

In John 14:1–21 we behold one great rainbow with six dimensions emanating from the heart of God to our hearts, then back from our hearts to Him. Each of the six "I will" promises is part of this glorious rainbow of the new covenant so we can know that we are loved to the uttermost and be empowered to love Him and one another to the utmost.

Christ came from the heart of God to reveal His love. The works He did were all an expression of this love. Love was the central motive of the healings, miracles, and signs He performed. And He called the disciples to continue His work. The first two "I will" promises were given to enable the disciples—and now to us—in loving Him and one another. The first promise is: "And whatever you ask in My name, that I will do, that the Father may be glorified in the Son." This "I will" is inseparably connected to the previous statement. "Most assuredly, I say to you, he who believes in Me, the works that I do he will do also; and greater works than these he will do, because I go to My Father." Praying in Christ's name, His purpose and power, is for "whatever" is needed to continue His ministry. The promise is not for our whims and wants, but for whatever needs we have in pressing forward with the works He did and the greater work of leading people to Him.

The second "I will" promise is connected to the challenge Christ gives in the verse that follows: "If you ask anything in My name, *I will do it.*" And then, "If you love Me, keep My commandments." Earlier that evening Christ had forcefully given His commandment—"A new commandment I give to you, that you love one another; as I have loved you, that you also love one another. By this all will know that you are My disciples, if you have love for one another" (John 13:34–35). The commandment defines what we are to pray for in Christ's name with boldness and confidence—love for Him, for one another in the fellowship of believers, and for people in the world who will be reached by Him through us.

We can't love like this on our own strength; we were never meant to. And this brings us to the next four "I will" promises. As Christ has told us to pray, now He tells us how

He will answer our prayers. As our Intercessor with the Father, He says, "And *I will pray* the Father, and He will give you another Helper, that He may abide with you forever—the Spirit of truth, whom the world cannot receive, because it neither sees Him nor knows Him; but you know Him, for He dwells with you and will be in you" (verses 16–17, italics added).

The Holy Spirit, who preexisted in oneness with the Father and the Son before creation and who had prepared the way for and was present during the ministry of the incarnate Christ, would now come to indwell in the disciples. What Christ promised happened at Pentecost. After His atoning cross and death-defeating resurrection, Christ ascended to be glorified and returned as the reigning Lord of the Church and as the baptizer with the Holy Spirit. He promised His disciples that He would pray for this in His "I will" promise, and it was answered.

One of the recipients of this prayer and the Father's answer was Peter. Filled with the Holy Spirit, Peter was inspired to explain the miracle of Pentecost: "This Jesus God has raised up, of which we are all witnesses. Therefore being exalted to the right hand of God, and having received from the Father the promise of the Holy Spirit, He poured out this which you now see and hear" (Acts 2:32–33).

Only after Pentecost were the disciples able to live the admonition to love the Lord and each other while doing the greater work of communicating their faith. The Holy Spirit was indeed their Helper. Christ called Him "another Helper." The word for *another* is *allos,* meaning "another of like kind." And the word for Helper is *Parakleton,* meaning "one who pleads a case for another, who stands beside to enable." As Christ is our Paraclete with the Father, so the Holy Spirit is Christ's Paraclete with us, convincing us of Christ's message, death, resurrection, and presence with us. Christ and the Holy Spirit are so much one in their ministry to us that we can say it is through the Holy

Spirit that Christ lives in us. As some put it, the Holy Spirit is Christ's other self, His alter ego, His abiding presence, the universalization of the Spirit of Christ in millions of believers throughout the world.

And this is how Christ fulfills the next two "I will" promises, which He promised to the disciples and to us the night before the cross. "I will not leave you orphans; I will come to you. A little while longer and the world will see Me no more, but you will see Me. Because I live, you will live also" (verses 18–19). The word for *orphans* is *orphanous,* meaning "desolate, bereft, lonely, unloved." Christ came to the disciples in post-resurrection appearances, and after Pentecost, through the Holy Spirit. But what about the promise that because He lives, we shall live also?

The astounding thing that occurred and continues to occur is a recapitulation of Christ's death and resurrection in the lives of men and women. A life-changing metamorphosis takes place. Through His cross a person not only receives forgiveness but becomes a new creature through a death to self and a resurrection to a new life. Indwelt by Christ through the Holy Spirit, a sweeping transformation takes place, producing a new person for whom physical death will only be a transition to heaven. Because Christ lives, we can live also at full potential in the abundant life He makes possible in ever-increasing power.

Then we are able to live in the reality of the rainbow of the new covenant: "At that day you will know that I am in My Father, and you in Me, and I in you" (verse 20). The Greek word for *know* is *gnosesthe,* from *ginosko,* which means "to know by experience and with assurance." The rainbow of the new covenant, Christ bringing to our hearts the love shared between Him and the Father, is the essence of life. Claiming and climbing this rainbow—we in Christ and Christ in us— we share in the mutual expression of eternal love. This is the prevenient source and the profound secret of loving the Lord and others.

Love for Keeps

When we claim these preceding five "I will" promises, we now have the power of His love to meet the condition stated in the sixth promise: "He who has My commandments and keeps them, it is he who loves *Me*. And he who loves *Me* will be loved by My Father, and I will love him and manifest Myself to him" (verse 21).

Note the way Christ enables what He expects. He gives us His commandment to love Him and one another. Then He tells us to ask for the power to do this. What He encourages us to ask for, He is ready to answer with the gift of love through the Holy Spirit. He will never leave us bereft of what we need. He makes it possible for us to overcome our basic egoistic selfishness through death to our old self and resurrection to a new, transformed person capable of receiving and giving authentic love.

By the Lord's grace we are prepared to meet His own qualifications of being able to receive this consistent flow of His love. We are able to keep His commandment to love because we are kept by His love . . . for keeps. His love for us always precedes our response of love for Him. But our response opens us to greater love from Him.

Now this sixth "I will" promise becomes our personal assurance. "I will love him and manifest Myself to him." We are back to where we started. We are able to hear and appropriate Christ's assurance, "I will always love you!"

Sometime after the resurrection and Pentecost, the church received into the fellowship one of Christ's brothers, Jude. He did not believe in the Lord during His incarnate ministry. We can only imagine what it might have been like for Jude to have the Savior sound in his soul, "I will always love you."

We are thankful that Jude heard this assurance. He became a leader in the Church. He wrote a short epistle that's long on wisdom. Two verses at the end always help me balance between keeping and being kept by the power of divine love: "*Keep* yourselves in the love of God, looking for the mercy of our Lord Jesus Christ unto eternal life. . . . Now to Him who is able to *keep* you from stumbling, / And to present you faultless / Before the presence of His glory with exceeding joy" (Jude 21, 24). We can keep ourselves in the love of God by focusing on this love as it is manifested to us by Jesus Christ because He is consistently able, has all power, to keep us from stumbling into the trap of trying to adequately love God in order to be loved by Him. And Christ does it by grace and mercy. When He presents us to the Father Christ is our advocate, and the Father loves us as He loves Him.

When will He present us faultless before God? Of course, at the end of our physical life when we go to heaven. But anyone who trusts the Savior daily in the pilgrimage of climbing the rainbow of the new covenant knows that Christ's hourly, moment-by-moment "I will always love you," keeps her or him from stumbling or turning back. We are surefooted only with Christ as the guide, showing us how to drive the stakes of His promises along the way. But this "I will" we're claiming, "I will love Him and manifest Myself to him," is the assurance of His presence beside us in the ascent. He ties us to Himself and shows us the next steps and the pitfalls to avoid or hides us in the cleft of His protection when avalanches of difficulties might throw us off the rainbow.

> He bound me with the cords of love
> And thus He bound me to Him

151

And round my heart still closely twines
The ties that naught can sever
For I am His and He is mine
Forever and forever.

Christ makes climbing the rainbow a daily, fresh source of grace by presenting us faultless before the presence of God's glory. "Here Father is My friend. Love him as You love Me!" We realize in part, but ever increasingly, the glory that we will behold at the end of our pilgrimage. This glory of God is the sum total of all His attributes in the radiant, shining majesty. And the rainbow of the new covenant we climb is itself the splendor of these attributes. As Christ whispers, "I will always love you," we know that among the attributes of God we experience through Him are loving kindness, faithfulness, and mercy.

We Don't Have to Paint Our Own Rainbow

While writing this book, a friend gave me a birthday card with a rainbow on the front. She knew I had rainbows on my mind. The message on the card was slightly off target. It said, "There's a rainbow ready for you to color and a heart waiting for your love . . . and all you need is the courage to do what you're dreaming of."

I am glad I don't have to color in the varying hues of the rainbow of the new covenant. This was done by Christ. Yes, there are hearts waiting for my love, but what a relief to know that my love is inadequate, like a riverbed with only a rivulet running through it, until Christ daily fulfills His promise, "Out of [your] heart will flow rivers of living waters" (John 7:38).

And as for the courage to press toward my dream of saying to the people of my life, "I will always love you!"—He alone can give me this courage. I repeatedly go over the six "I wills," confirming Christ's willingness to help me provide this daily measure of courage.

- Accept Christ's commandment to love Him and others.

- Ask for whatever I need to keep that commandment.

- Receive His answer in the gift of the Holy Spirit and claim supernatural power to love as a fruit of the Spirit.

- Assume that Christ will never leave me as an orphan, I am an adopted son in the Father's family growing daily in my likeness to my Elder Brother.

- Rejoice in the astounding miracle of being raised out of the living death of selfishness to a deathless life of giving myself to others.

- Praise Christ constantly for introducing me to the glory of the Father's heart, and worship His majesty in the splendor of His attributes.

- Look for and expect Christ's interventions with the renewed anointing of the Holy Spirit giving assurance of grace and special courage for the need of the hour.

John Donne said, "When God loves, He loves to the end; and not only their own end, to their death, but to His end, and His end is, that He might love them still." And to this end, Christ says, "I will always love you!"

10

Distracting Comparisons

If I will that he remain till I come, what is that to you? You follow Me.

John 21:22

*T*here's a terrible virus going around. Many of us have caught it. And we're guilty of spreading it to others.

This particular strain of virus is especially complicated and difficult to cure. It causes blurred vision, agitated emotions, depression, and a depleted self-image.

The virus attacks us spiritually as well as confuses our thinking and our attitudes. I'm calling it "the virus of distracting comparisons."

Symptoms of this virus are fairly easy to diagnose, though we try to hide them. We measure ourselves by comparing ourselves to others rather than enjoying the unique, special miracle Christ has called each of us to be and is working night and day to help us become.

An Old Friend with the Virus

I met an old friend on a cross-country flight recently who was really suffering from a fresh infection of the virus of distracting comparisons. He seemed to be very down, and I tried to find out why.

"Oh, I don't know," he said, even though I suspected he did know. After a long pause it all came out.

"I spent last week at a convention. There were dozens of my old classmates there. It really got to me when I saw all that they've accomplished, all their advanced degrees and titles, their significant jobs, and all they've acquired. The more I talked with them the sadder I felt about my life and how little I had to show for all the hard work."

I was surprised. The man has really done very well with his career and family. But the virus of distracting comparisons causes a self-depreciation whenever we meet someone who has seemingly outdistanced us in the rat race.

Ever Happen to You?

Has this spiritual virus ever attacked you? Ever look around at your friends, neighbors, siblings, or an old classmate or fellow worker from the past and wondered why some seem to have a corner on success and prosperity? There's always someone who can do better at what we've worked hard to do well. It's hard not to make comparisons.

But these self-measurements against others cause an irritating static in our souls. The static interferes with the Lord's clear signal of His plan for each of us. This signal that's constantly being beamed to our souls gets scrambled when we compare our physical looks, intelligence quotient, or abilities with anyone else. And who hasn't tuned out the Lord for a spell of covetous, whining comparisons? "I've worked as hard as that guy. Why don't I have a home like his?"

Often we are egged on to buy something simply because someone else has it. Ever think that your old car seems particularly run down after seeing a friend in his or her shiny new one? And our wardrobe never seems more out of style than when we see someone in a smashing new outfit. The virus of distracting comparisons saps us of our spiritual nourishment.

The old Spanish proverb is right: "Envy is always thin; it bites but never eats."

Fever Proportions

This virus reaches fever proportions when we start evaluating how the Lord has dealt with us in comparison to others. A tough time of problems or even suffering makes us wonder about God when others seem to have an easy road. Some seem to be suntanned with blessing while others are pale by comparison. And we question why some have been exempted from the physical or emotional pain we have endured. We want to shout, "Why me?"

The virus threatens our peace of mind when we compare our spiritual experiences with others'. Some people seem to be given greater inspiration, gifts, opportunities. And when they talk about their insights or discoveries we wonder, "Where was I when all those blessings were being handed out?" These kinds of comparisons take our eyes off the Lord and put them on other people. The result is that we get bound up in the little package of ourselves, feeling frustrated and discontented.

A Storm Inside While the Skies Are Blue

Simon Peter had a bad case of distracting comparison early one morning. When the resurrected Lord came to him and the disciples beside the Sea of Galilee the sky was crystal blue, but a storm of remorse raged inside him because he had denied the Master during His trial before the crucifixion. Peter wept bitterly every time he thought of it. Even the joy of the Lord's post-resurrection appearances in the Upper Room had not healed the pain of his regret. Peter did the very thing he so jauntily protested he would never do.

Competitive comparisons had always been his problem, Peter thought. He constantly elbowed himself above his friends and now he had done it again and failed miserably. Here he was, standing around the breakfast fire on the shore with the risen Lord and the other disciples. Eventually the others drifted away, perhaps sensing that Peter and the Lord had something they needed to talk about privately. Everyone knew what it was and that it had to be resolved. Only John lingered close by, listening for how the Lord would part the clouds in Simon Peter's stormy soul.

The Lord cut right to the raw nerve in Simon Peter. "Simon, do you love Me more than these?" pointing, I surmise, at the other disciples. A tough question. Especially when we note in the Greek that the strongest word for *love* is used (*agapais* from the verb *agapao*), expressing deep, loyal, faithful love. An unselfish love, ready to serve. Simon's response, "Yes, Lord; You know that I love You," has a different word for love in the Greek text (*philo* from *phileo*), expressing tender, cherishing affection, and friendship. The disciple's response might be better translated, "Yes, Lord, You know that I am Your friend." And to this the Lord gives Peter the first of three recalls to service, "Feed My lambs."

Then Christ repeats the same question a second time. We feel the Lord probing to the inner recesses of Peter's heart to ensure that he had the humility that would be necessary for non-competitive spiritual leadership in the future. Once again Peter responds with caution, not using the Lord's word for love but attesting to hero-attachment, an affection of friendship. Peter knew that he hadn't expressed loyal love before when he had denied Christ. One thing he knew for sure—he wanted to be counted as Christ's friend. To Peter's guarded response again came another recall: "Tend My sheep."

It's fascinating to note that Christ's third question utilizes the word for love that Peter had used in his response to Jesus' first two questions. The Lord really pushed the vacillating disciple. The third question Christ asked could be interpreted, "Simon, are you really My friend? You have professed your ties to Me, but are you ready to serve Me by serving others?" This time Peter was cut to the heart. John, who was close by, records that Peter was grieved. Peter's answer indicates that he was pressed to the edge, "Lord, You know all things; You know that I love You." Again, the same word for love. It was the best the disciple could say. He was trying hard not to say more than he was sure he could produce. Now Christ's third recall to service was, "Feed My sheep." A threefold recall for a threefold denial. Christ knows how to heal guilt with remedial restitution!

When Christ continued it was to drive home the point He wanted to make. Peter was recalled to the sacrificial love of Christ, the kind he would need during the trials ahead. Yes, there would be the joy of the high adventure He had promised, but Peter would die a martyr's death. "Most assuredly, I say to you, when you were younger, you girded yourself and walked where you wished; but when you are old, you will stretch out your hands, and another will gird you and carry you where you do not wish. . . . Follow Me" (John 21:18–19). The obvious implication is that Peter would be crucified.[1]

It's hard to imagine how Peter reacted to what Christ told him. Instead of responding to the awesome prophecy the Lord had given him about his martyr's death, Peter's only thought was a distracting comparison. He looked over at John, the disciple who had always seemed closest to Christ. Was it an old flare-up of competition, even jealousy, that prompted Peter to want to know what would be required for John? Would he get off easier? Expressing the same old problem that caused his trouble before, Peter blurted out the most incongruous of non sequiturs ever spoken. It didn't fit, nor did it follow. Pointing to John, Peter said in a demanding tone: "But what about this man?"

I have reviewed the account of what happened that morning alongside the Sea of Galilee to see a very illuminating example of distracting comparisons in its full context of Peter's character development. This brought forth one of the most forceful "I will" assertions, which, when understood is a very hopeful rainbow for those of us whose lives are continually plagued by this virus. I think it was the turning point for Peter when he surrendered the future management of his life to Christ and stopped trying to control Him.

Peter's Rainbow and Ours

Christ's commanding, decisive, authoritative response to Peter has the divine ring of the soon-to-be-glorified reigning Lord of the church. In this "I will" He expresses the authority of His will and therefore what will be done through His control over the lives of people. That's why this "I will" assertion was so important for Peter and for us. Picking up on Peter's imperious questioning of how his destiny would compare with John's, Christ sharply rebuked Peter for meddling in what He alone would decide. The Lord said flatly, "If I will that he should remain till I come, what is that to you? You follow Me" (John 21:22).

In modern vernacular, Christ's direct, stern response would be, "That's none of your business! Put your eyes on Me and take them off of John. Stop comparing yourself to him or to anybody else. I'll decide what I will for John and what I will for you. You'll be the apostle I plan for you to be when you stop trying to run your own and everyone else's life and give Me the control of your life and future."

Why do I call this a rainbow promise? Because it gives us the assurance that Christ is the Lord of our future and can get our "selves" off of our hands and into His capable hands. It breaks through the dark, rainy, moody clouds of our distracting comparisons that make so much of life turbulent and gives us a chance of a new beginning.

Now let's consider why this "I will" assertion is so crucial for our future effectiveness and joy.

1. It Puts Our Attention Where It Belongs

In this forceful statement Christ has called us to put our focus on Him and not on other people. If we are to make comparisons they should be between us and Him. He alone can be an adequate example for us. And the startling news is that you and I were programmed for greatness by making Him our magnificent obsession. This was Paul's secret, "For to me, to live is Christ" (Phil 1:21). "I have been crucified with Christ; it is no longer I who live but Christ lives in me; and the life which I now live in the flesh I live by faith in the Son of God, who loved me and gave Himself for me" (Gal. 2:20); "I can do all things through Christ who strengthens me" (Phil 4:13).

The point is—any time or energy spent in comparisons with other people, either in pride because we think we're better or in envy because we covet their talents or opportunities, that much less time we have for really concentrating on Christ and what we were meant to become in Him.

2. It Keeps Us from Missing Our Uniqueness

Jesus Christ has enlisted us to be a unique miracle of His grace. Walt Whitman used to say, "I celebrate myself." This is off target. We can say, "I celebrate the new person Christ is molding me to be. He's the Potter; I'm the clay." Christ has a purpose for everything we experience; everything happens in order for us to become the people He has in mind. Distracting comparisons keep us from celebrating the evolving new persons we are becoming.

I like to read 2 Corinthians 5:17 with personal emphasis through first-person-singular pronouns. First here's how it reads in The Living Bible: "When someone becomes a Christian he becomes a brand new person inside. He is not the same anymore. A new life has begun!" Now here's how it can read as our personal affirmation: "When I became a Christian I became a brand new person inside. I'm not the same anymore. A new life has begun!"

We can't experience this if our attention is distracted by comparing ourselves to how Christ is creating His new creation in someone else. Thoreau spoke of marching to a different drummer. However, our Drummer is Christ, and we are to follow His drumbeat.

Of course, we all have people we admire and who inspire us. There are things about them we want to emulate. This is fine if they are Christ-character traits that He can also reproduce in us. We were meant to be mimics of Christ, not cookie-cutter cutouts of someone else.

You are a wonder. Christ is blessing you uniquely and distinctly for what He intends you to be.

There's another reason this "I will" assertion is a powerful rainbow to end the overcast clouds of comparisons.

3. It Emphasizes Christ's Personal Will for Us

Our Lord has a personal will for each of us, a will that includes all of the elements of His overall will for all Christians. But it also has specific direction for each of our lives, and that is not intended for anybody else. He has plans for every person.

This was why Peter's presumptuous demand to compare the Lord's will for John with His will for him was not only arrogant but irrelevant. Christ had plans for Peter much greater than he could imagine that day beside the Sea of Galilee. But the Lord does not outline the specifics of His will for the future so we can compare them with what He wills for others. His primary will is that we know and love Him, follow in however much light He gives us, and leave the unfolding of the future to Him.

The Lord wants us to be content in Him. He does not want us to gloat or grouse about His personal will for us in comparison with His strategy for others.

In fact, Christ used Peter and John in different ways. Both of them illuminate the wonderful way the Lord uses very different kinds of people to do His work. Peter was a man of action, always eager, often impulsive, but consistently ardent in friendship with Christ that grew into the *leal* (the Scottish word for loyal) love that motivated his servant ministry. The remarkable change in Peter came at Pentecost, when the reigning Christ baptized him with the Holy Spirit. Peter became the pivotal spokesperson and leader of the church of Jerusalem. Christ's promise that the disciples would do the works that He had done—and greater works—was fulfilled, especially in Peter. The vacillator became the rock that Christ had designated him to be.

The salient benchmark quality that Peter displayed as the church grew was his apparent freedom from comparisons. He was able to affirm the eventual shift of primary leadership from him to James in the Jerusalem church and to Paul in the expansion of Christianity to the Gentile world. Though his role in the conversion of Cornelius and his subsequent affirmation of opening the church to Gentile converts was decisive, his ministry was primarily winning Jews to Christ as Messiah and Lord. It is very significant, however, that near the end of his life in Rome about A.D. 64 Peter wrote two letters to both Gentile and Jewish believers in Asia Minor who were suffering persecution from Nero.

These Christians were mainly converts through the ministry of the Apostle Paul and were members of a church founded and nurtured by Paul. At no point does Peter begrudge another apostle's ministry, but lifts up Christ as he instructs the believers in the depths of Christian experience and to sublime heights of Christian hope. It was around A.D. 67 that Peter was martyred in Rome. Peter died knowing that he had done what Christ called him to do and that the evangelization of the world would go on through others uniquely called to take up where he had left off.

John is no less an illustration of how Christ can transform a person with a comparison complex. Nonbiblical descriptions of him have been misleading. We have misrepresented this competitive firebrand by depicting him as a delicate, beardless dreamer. What he became after the resurrection and the Pentecost only intensifies our amazement over the man he was and the transformed person he became. We forget the disciple John during Jesus' Galilean ministry who consistently jockeyed for a place closest to the Master. John even sent his mother to approach Jesus with the recommendation that he be given a place of honor at Christ's right hand when He came to His kingly power. It was John who wanted Jesus to rain down fire on a Samaritan village when its people rejected Him on the way to Jerusalem. John's personality matched the sea on which he sailed. He knew tender moments of calm interrupted by tempestuous storms, tornadoes of anger, and swells of impetuous outbursts. There brewed within John a compound of ambition, jealousy, conceit, thin-skinned sensitivity, and a violent temper.

John's second name became "the disciple whom Jesus loved." This says more about John's neediness rather than any preferential treatment from the Master. John's experience of Jesus' crucifixion and resurrection started a personality transformation that was climaxed when he received power at Pentecost. Through the indwelling of the Holy Spirit, John experienced a closeness and oneness with Christ that exceeded anything he knew before or immediately after the resurrection. Christ became John's abiding, empowering companion. Christ was life for John.

This is good news for you and me. Christ can change human nature. It's encouraging to see the difference between John the disciple and John the apostle. After Pentecost and during the first years of the early church, we see him as a leader whose eyes were focused on Christ and not on confusing comparisons. This is why Christ could use John so mightily.

Life for John was not easy or placid through the years. Hardship, persecution, and suffering punctuated his days. But through it all, abiding in Christ and Christ abiding in him, was the secret of John's effectiveness. From the exciting days of the expansion of the church that brought him to Ephesus, to his imprisonment on Patmos as a political prisoner, to prolonged ministry in the Lycus Valley and throughout Asia Minor, John's vision of Christ was the center and source of life for him.

In John we see an immense intelligence and theological perceptiveness under the control and maximizing power of the Holy Spirit. Steeped in his Hebrew background, fortified by his first-hand experience of Christ's life, crucifixion and resurrection, nurtured by years of life abiding in the risen, reigning Christ and sensitive to the unfulfilled quest of Greek philosophy—John wrote his stunning Gospel under the guidance of the Spirit. It reads like the work of a converted Hebrew scholar schooled in Greek philosophy. His epistles and Revelation are equally stimulating intellectually and spiritually. In them we meet the preexistent Logos, who speaks with *I am,* Yahweh authority, the light of the world, the only Savior and *the* truth, the Lord of lords. All from the Holy Spirit-inspired pen of a fisherman who claimed his own special calling and destiny.

I'm glad John didn't spend his life comparing himself to Paul or Peter or Timothy. It was the Lord's plan for John to live a long and fruitful life.

There's a lovely story about John in the last year of his life. He had to be carried into a meeting of the church of Ephesus. Though he was frail in body, his faith and spirit were indomitable. His message was predictable. With a strong, unwavering voice he said, "Little children, love one another."

It is said that a bright, but impetuous young deacon asked, "Why do you always repeat the same message?" John's response was, "That's all you need to know."

4. Jesus' "I Will" Assertion Is Also a Challenge to Care and Not Compare

As long as we are distracted by comparisons with other people we are not able to love them. They become objects of competition rather than people who have needs. Christ's strong "You follow Me!" at the end of this statement calls us to follow His commandment to love. When we evaluate people, longing for what they are able to do or have, while at the same time looking for their faults to see ourselves in a better light, we don't really love them. Nor do we empathize with their hurts and hopes. And least of all, we are not open to receive what they may be able to do to help us grow. This would be further proof that they have what we do not have.

"What a miserable way to live!" you say. I agree. So why do we? Why continue to live under these clouds of comparisons with a lifetime of monsoons of either self-aggrandizement or self-pity? Our calling is to care for people, not to compare ourselves with them.

168

So, here are the mallet blows to drive this crucial stake of security while climbing the rainbow of the new covenant in Christ:

Put your attention on Christ.

Celebrate your own uniqueness.

Accept Christ's special will for you.

Affirm other people.

The View from the Summit

We have reached the summit. We have climbed the rainbow to the highest point we can reach in this portion of our eternal life. As we have claimed some of the most salient "I will" promises of the Lord, we have climbed to the place where we can behold His glory.

One final "I will" promise holds us secure on the summit. It is a promise of our eternal destiny that in a sublime way can be experienced now. The promise offers us both the perspective and the power of Christ for the role we are to assume as His disciples. This awesome invitation was first made to the church at Laodicea by the risen, reigning Christ. "To him who overcomes I will grant to sit with Me on My throne, as I also overcame and sat down with My Father on His throne" (Rev. 3:21).

We often think of this promise as one we will realize only when we graduate to heaven. And yet, what is offered in fullest measure then can begin now. This promise, like all those made at the end of the messages of the risen Christ to the churches of Asia Minor in Revelation 2 and 3, is made to those who claim the overcoming, conquering victory of Christ in this life. There's no reason to assume this startling promise to the church at Laodicea is any different and limited only to life after physical death. These words of the living Lord are in sync with the divine inspiration of the apostle Paul's message to the Ephesians. Note the *now* intensity of Ephesians 2:4–6, affirming the same perspective and authority given to Christianity today, "But God, who is rich in mercy, because of His great love with which He loves us, even when we were dead in trespasses, made us alive together with Christ (by grace you have been saved) and raised us up together, and *made us sit together in the heavenly places in Christ Jesus.*" The "heavenly places" means the unseen world of spiritual reality.

And the place we sit is with Christ on His throne. What does His throne mean? It means ruling with authority and power. To sit with Christ is to be delegated to share His kingdom authority and receive His power. While on earth we are given the perspective of Christ on our daily struggles. We are lifted above our pressures to be able to see them from His point of view. In prayer He shows us what He is seeking to do for us to make us overcomers. He also reveals His will for the world around us and gives His authority to act boldly and fearlessly. The panic about life and its challenges and frightening possibilities we've talked about throughout this book can now be like a shabby old garment we take off and never need to put on again.

Picture your life as one around the throne of Christ. No need for comparisons or competition there. You are one in mind and spirit with the Lord's chosen covenant people. And as you boldly approach Christ with your petitions, He gives you His eyes to envision what He sees is best. Then you hear His commanding voice, "Do this in My Name, all authority in heaven and earth is given to Me. Do not be afraid, I will give you My power to accomplish what I have assigned to you!"

What the apostle John saw around the throne now we see: "A rainbow around the throne, in appearance like an emerald!" We have climbed the rainbow of the covenant to the summit and now see that it reaches to its source in the rainbow of glory around the throne. From this vantage we can face any storm in the future. The rainbow is now in our hearts.

Changing the tense of George Matheson's line, we can say, sing, and shout with joy:

> I *have* climbed the rainbow in the rain
> And *know* the promises are not in vain!

Notes

Chapter 1 • Climbing the Rainbow

1. D. Macwilliam, *The Life of George Matheson* (London: Hodder and Stoughton, 1907), 181.

2. Quoted in John Crew Taylor, *The Blind Seer, George Matheson* (London: Vision Prose, 1960), 170. Portions of this quote may be traced to a sermon by James Black that is included in his book, *Days of My Autumn* (London: Hodder and Stoughton), 223.

Chapter 2 • The Reach Across the Breach

1. Sarah Doudney, "The Hardest Time of All," from *The Light of the World: Poems of Faith and Consolation*, comp. Joseph Morris and St. Clair Adams (New York: George Sully and Co., 1928), 64.

Chapter 6 • The Longing to Escape When the Going Gets Rough

1. John Steinbeck, *Travels with Charley: In Search of America* (New York: Viking Press, 1962), 24.

Chapter 10 • Distracting Comparisons

1. Actually, when Peter was executed by Rome, the apostle insisted that he be crucified upside down so there would be no confusion between his martyr's death and Christ's atoning crucifixion for the sins of the world.